Fabulous Fat Quarter Bags

A gorgeous gathering of bags for every day

Susan Briscoe

David and Charles

www.mycraftivity.com

For my patchwork and quilting friends

A DAVID & CHARLES BOOK
Copyright © David & Charles Limited 2009

David & Charles is an F+W Media Inc. company
4700 East Galbraith Road
Cincinnati, OH 45236

First published in the UK and USA in 2009

Text and illustrations copyright © Susan Briscoe 2009

A catalogue record for this book is available from the
British Library.

ISBN-13: 978-0-7153-2979-5 hardback
ISBN-10: 0-7153-2979-0 hardback

ISBN-13: 978-0-7153-2978-8 paperback
ISBN-10: 0-7153-2978-2 paperback

Printed in China by RR Donnelly
for David & Charles
Brunel House   Newton Abbot   Devon

Commissioning Editor: Jane Trollope
Desk Editor: Emily Rae
Project Editor: Cathy Joseph
Art Editor: Sarah Clark
Designer: Joanna Ley
Production Controller: Ros Napper

Visit our website at www.davidandcharles.co.uk

David & Charles books are available from all good
bookshops; alternatively you can contact our Orderline
on 0870 9908222 or write to us at FREEPOST EX2
110, D&C Direct, Newton Abbot, TQ12 4ZZ (no stamp
required UK only); US customers call 800-289-0963 and
Canadian customers call 800-840-5220.

Contents

Introduction

Fat quarters and patchwork bags are, quite simply, made for each other. The handy size of a quartered yard (or metre), a squarish piece of fabric approximately 18in x 21in (50cm x 54cm), is suited to a small project. Practically a unit of fabric currency in the quilting world, they are temptingly displayed in neatly folded boxes and baskets at quilt shops and shows. Better still, they are sold as coordinating bundles, tied with strings or ribbons – just the thing for a gift or treat. You can indulge a whim for colours and designs you like but might not use for a larger project, creating a unique yet practical patchwork bag in the process – once you have finished stroking and admiring the beautifully coloured fat quarters in your hands!

Using a variety of numbers of fat quarters in a bundle as my starting point, from just two fat quarters through to eight, I've designed a new collection of bags, each with a smaller purse or accessory. Just for fun, there's a set for every day of the week.

For each bag and accessory duo I've shown the finished projects in alternative fat quarter fabrics to create a completely different style. Monday's Strippy Handbag and Wedge Purse come in sophisticated African prints or bright and cheerful batiks, for example. Take the Eclipse Bag and Celestial Circles Purse out for a sparkly evening on Tuesday or go sixties mod for retro shopping. On Wednesday, the Laptop Bag and Gadget Pocket have a bold, urban style or choose floral prints for a creative mood. In minimalist monochrome, Thursday's Typo Satchel and Book Bag are just the business for business, or maybe it's your time to relax with a day off work in cool taupe style. By Friday you might need to shop for more fabric with the blue, turquoise and gold Swag Bag and Curvy Coin Purse, or go country chic at the farmers' market. The Quilter's Suitcase and Mini Pochette are perfect for a Saturday quilt workshop in brilliant Japanese prints, but more sophisticated in khaki coordinates for a weekend city break. Hop on a plane with Sunday's Pick and Mix Backpack and Ticket Pocket in warm, autumnal tones, or take to the sea with nautical blues.

Every bag and accessory are designed to be 'fat quarter friendly'. Of course, you can use more fabrics or your scrap bag bits, if you wish, and there might be a fat quarter bundle in your fabric stash that could be combined with another fabric that you haven't used yet.

Each bag and accessory duo shares the same patchwork technique, which is different every time. I've used easy but effective patchwork and appliqué techniques for good results that will really make the most of your fabrics. If you wish, you can try out the technique on the smaller project before making the larger one or, as I did, make the smaller project with the fabric leftovers from its big sister.

All of the larger bags and some of the smaller ones use the quilter's favourite finishing method, bias binding. It simplifies construction, giving the bags shape without the need for heavy stiffeners and keeping them soft to sew. Instructions are provided to add zips, handles and straps to the bags and you can complete the look by embellishing with buttons, charms, beads, braid or lace … pretty, practical and perfectly yours.

Using this book

- All fabric sizes include seam allowances.
- Labelling the bags with days of the week is just for fun – some bags will take longer than a day to make!
- Wadding (batting) and backing fabric sizes are cut slightly larger than required and trimmed to size after quilting, so they will be bigger than your patchwork panels.
- Actual sizes are given for cord, braid, zips and so-on. There is no need to add on any extra allowance.
- Machine sew means with a straight stitch, unless otherwise stated. Start and finish all bag seams by reverse stitching for ½in (1.2cm).
- Some pattern pieces need to be enlarged on a photocopier, but some simpler, larger pieces can be drafted.

Equipment

If you are a quilter, you will probably have most of the equipment you need for making patchwork bags. No specialist gadgets are needed and many items will be found in your sewing basket if you are a dressmaker or sew soft furnishings. Check that you have the following items to hand before you start making your chosen bag, so you don't have to stop and hunt for things!

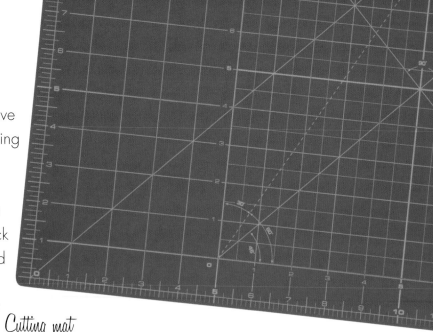

Cutting mat

You must use a self-healing cutting mat with your rotary cutter, to protect your table and make sure your cutter blade stays sharp. Choose a mat marked with imperial or metric measurements, depending on which you intend to use throughout the book. You can use the measurements on the mat to help you cut larger pieces but check your mat and ruler measurements are exactly the same.

Rotary cutter

Rotary cutting has made fabric cutting easier than ever, speeding it up and enabling you to machine sew an exact ¼in (6mm) seam with the quarter inch foot (using the cut fabric edge as a guide). Dull, nicked blades will skip threads and make cutting difficult (keep a spare blade handy). All cutters have a blade set at the end of a handle with a safety guard, see Cutting safety, page 12.

Quilter's ruler

This transparent, wider-than-normal ruler marked with a grid is an indispensable tool, both for rotary cutting and for marking quilting patterns in straight lines. Imperial quilt rulers are divided into inches and fractions of an inch, to ⅛in. Metric rulers are marked in centimetres, half centimetres and millimetres. Many have 45- and 60-degree lines too, useful for cutting fabric on the bias. Rulers 4½in and 6½in wide are the most useful for projects in this book. Select a ruler with clear markings.

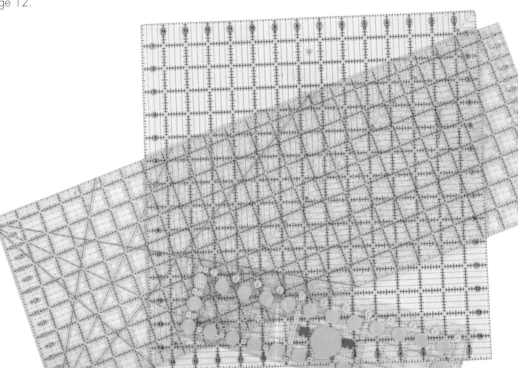

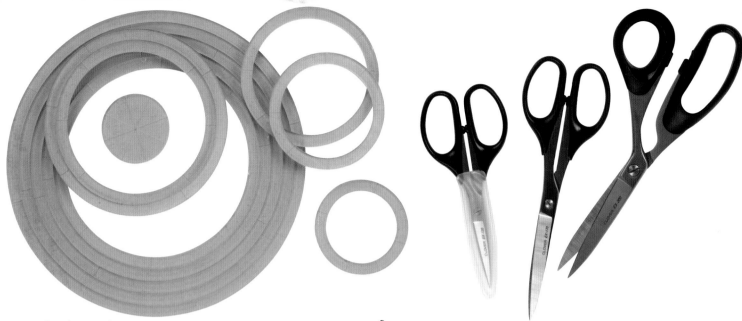

Circle templates

Use these to draw shapes for bags or round off corners of bag panels. Make your own from cardboard or template plastic, or buy a stacking set of acrylic circular templates.

Scissors

A large pair of sewing scissors is required for cutting out curves, cutting braid and similar tasks. Reserve your best quality sewing scissors for fabric. Use your 'second best' pair for cutting wadding (batting), as this can dull the blades. A small pair of embroidery scissors or thread snips makes trimming threads easy. Use paper scissors for cutting out paper templates for quilting panels.

Sewing machine

You will need a reliable lockstitch sewing machine that can sew straight stitches and zigzag. Utility stitches and a small range of embroidery stitches are also useful. There are a number of domestic machines made for quilters that are supplied with specialized presser feet (see picture right) and a range of stitches useful for quilting.

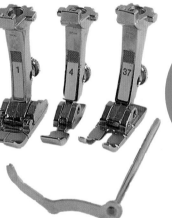

Use the correct foot for the stitch and test tension on a scrap of fabric before you begin. A walking foot (not illustrated) is necessary for smooth straight-line machine quilting. It synchronises with the feed dogs to 'walk' all the layers in the quilt sandwich through at the same rate so the patchwork top doesn't distort or form ridges. To avoid wobbly quilting lines, change the throat plate to a straight stitch plate – the zigzag throat plate has a slot for the needle to move up and down to the bobbin race but a straight stitch plate only has a hole, so any hint of a zigzag is removed. You must remember to change back to the zigzag plate before trying to stitch any sideways stitch patterns.

Use an appropriate machine needle for your work and change it frequently – immediately if damaged or bent or if your machine starts skipping stitches. A 'microtex' needle size 80/12 is good for patchwork. A quilting needle is designed to stitch through several layers of fabric and wadding (batting), so it is ideal for bag assembly as well as quilting – use a 75/11 for quilting and a 90/14 for bag assembly.

Most modern machines have a 'free arm' feature, where the flat machine extension table can be removed. The free arm can make handling curved sections of bags easier.

TIP

If you are using a specialist thread for quilting, match the needle to the thread type – metallic, embroidery and jeans needles all have larger eyes to sew threads that would snap in a regular quilting.

Other useful items

- An iron and an ironing board for pressing patchwork and bag assembly (see Pressing patchwork, page 14). Use a steam iron and pressing cloth to press bag assembly seams after each stage of construction.
- A seam ripper or quick unpick for removing tacking (basting) after inserting zips or for unpicking mistakes – remove a stitch at a time.
- A tape measure for checking measurements.
- Fabric markers to mark some sewing lines in bag assembly and also to mark quilting patterns. You will need markers in a variety of colours to contrast with your fabrics so that they can be easily seen and removed. Tailor's chalk, quilter's marking pencils and Chaco liners (chalk wheels) are available in several colours.
- Sharps hand sewing needles, for tacking pieces together or finishing off bias bound edges.
- Quilting pins, for assembling bags, are long and fine, usually with a glass head. Pin at right angles to the seam you are sewing. They can also be used for pin basting the quilt sandwich. Fine, slightly flexible silk pins are good for pinning the curved sections of smaller bags.
- Hole punch pliers and eyelet setting pliers (or a setting tool and a small hammer) to set the ¼in (6mm) eyelets for the Typo Satchel and Book Bag straps.

Materials

Fat quarters, either sold individually or in coordinated bundles, are the main pre-cut size sold in most quilt shops. Finding a good range of fat quarters will be easy, especially with the number of quilt shops now doing mail order, selling over the Internet or at larger quilt shows. Once you've decided on your fabrics, you can select fasteners and trims to achieve a coordinated look.

Fabrics

There are thousands of cotton fabrics now in production specially for patchwork. Cotton is best as it is easy to cut and press with a sharp crease. Designers and manufacturers produce fully coordinated fabric ranges on a seasonal basis and with a high turnover akin to high street fashion, so if you see a fabric you really like, buy it while you can! Most collections have several colour variations for each pattern and will include large and small-scale prints.

- Large prints or feature fabrics can give lots of pattern variety from one fabric. They are often the most obviously eye-catching designs in a collection.
- Small prints or mini prints act as a great foil to the larger designs, playing a supporting role without competing for too much attention.
- Tone-on-tone prints are useful as an alternative to plains and as a transition between patterns. They can reinforce the main fabric theme while being calm and unobtrusive.
- Directional prints include motifs arranged in stripes or rows, or with an obvious 'right way up'. If there are pictorial elements in the design, plan carefully so they aren't upside-down.

Many designers include stripes, checks or spots in their ranges, especially for retro or country style.

- Stripes, woven or printed, add structure and a sense of movement to your patchwork. You can follow the lines in your quilting if you wish, or play with arranging the stripes in a particular direction within the patchwork.
- Checks and plaids can be woven or printed. They will add a sense of movement when used on the diagonal while calming the design when used straight.
- Spots and dots can be lively or subtle, depending on the colour contrast and size of the dots. They are best used with other prints, as too many dots can be overwhelming.

Patterned fabrics are easy to coordinate with plain cottons, dyed after weaving and produced in dozens of colours. Other patchwork fabrics include metallic prints, with gold, silver or copper highlights that add sparkle, usually on top of a printed or dyed design, and batiks, with shaded colour changes across the fabric, in many different colours.

Other fabrics

Backing fabric: in the quilt 'sandwich' this is behind the wadding (batting). The backing shows on the reverse of a patchwork quilt but is hidden in bags by the linings, so it doesn't need to coordinate with the patchwork. A soft, good quality, pre-shrunk natural calico is ideal for all the bags in this book.

Lining fabric: linings protect the back of the patchwork and quilting from being rubbed by the bag's contents. Plainer, less 'busy' prints are good as heavy patterns can camouflage the contents, especially in handbags. You can use several different fabrics for the lining, continuing the patchwork theme inside your bags.

Denim and heavier fabrics: although not suitable for patchwork, I chose tough denim (non stretch) and thicker cottons for the base sections of the Typo Satchel, the Quilter's Suitcase and the Pick and Mix Backpack. Canvas, needlecord, faux suede and lightweight furnishing fabric could also be used.

Bias binding

The coordinating bias binding used to finish many bags is made from one of the fat quarters in the bundle. See Making bias binding, page 18.

Pre-washing fabrics

Many quilters pre-wash all the fabrics if they are making a quilt, so that they don't run or shrink the first time the quilt is washed. If you want to be able to wash your bag without risk, give your fat quarters a quick machine wash to flush out any excess dye and pre-shrink the fabric (make sure that all your fabrics are washable, including any thicker fabrics used for the bag base). Starch and press the dried fabrics to make them easier to use. Leather handles and wooden buttons can't be washed without spoiling their finish so remove from a bag before washing and replace afterwards.

Fat quarter bundles

Many quilt shops sell fabrics packed in coordinated fat quarter bundles. Sometimes these come straight from the manufacturer but more often they are selected and packed in store. They may include fabrics from the same range or be selected across several ranges that the shop staff know will work well together. A typical bundle will include an assortment of the fabrics listed above or may include just one type (plains, shot cottons and batiks are often presented in a homogenous bundle).

Bundles may include any number of fat quarters from two upwards, sometimes with an entire range in one bundle – too much for one bag. Too few or too many fat quarters aren't a problem as you can always add more fat quarters using the bundles as a starting point or split it up for several projects.

Threads for quilting and appliqué

All the bags are machine quilted, with easy designs. Try multicoloured machine quilting threads to accent your patchwork, like the grid design on the Quilter's Suitcase. For quilting 'in the ditch', along the seam line, choose a thread that blends with the fabrics, as used for the Typo Satchel. Quilting with a fancy machine stitch, like the floral scroll pattern used on the Swag Bag, will show up well so long as there is enough contrast between the thread and fabric – you don't need a fancy thread to contribute to the overall design.

Threads for patchwork and bag assembly

Use good quality cotton thread for sewing patchwork and for bag assembly, with softer tacking (basting) threads for temporary stitching. Dull or neutral colours, like brown, sage green, dark blue, grey and beige are the most useful for patchwork, coordinating with most colour mixtures. Don't use polyester as a general sewing thread because it is stronger than the cotton fibres and can eventually cut through fabric.

Wadding (batting)

Bags use small pieces of wadding (batting), so off-cuts left over from larger quilting projects will often be large enough for a bag panel. Otherwise, quilt wadding is sold in standard sizes and by the yard (metre). Wadding is made in various natural and manmade fibres. I used an 80 per cent cotton, 20 per cent polyester blended wadding for the bags, but 100 per cent cotton wadding would be suitable as well. Cotton and cotton blends cling between the patchwork and backing so are easier to machine quilt than polyester wadding, which tends to slip instead. Thin 2oz wadding is best as thicker wadding will make the bag seams bulky and difficult to sew.

Embellishments

Several of the bags are decorated with embellishments, chosen with the fabric choice as the key, such as the Laptop Bag with a full set of typewriter brads laid out as a keyboard. Many charms, embellishments and buttons are sold for patchwork projects but think creatively and check out scrap-booking and other crafts for useable novelties.

Fasteners and other notions

Different bag designs suit different kinds of fasteners, buckles and trims. Several bags are closed with zips inserted using the easy method described on page 17. The same fastener can suit two different fabric themes, like the decorative antique brass cloak clasps for both Laptop Bags. Try coordinating different notions for each fat quarter selection, like the Typo Satchel and Book Bag's chrome buckles and eyelets. Plastic buckles can match fabric or webbing colours, such as the red plastic slide-release buckles for the main Pick and Mix Backpack and dark blue plastic tri-glide slide buckles for the alternative.

Straps, handles and webbing

Ready-made straps and handles are widely available and give a professional look to your bags. Leather straps come in various lengths and colours. The ones I use need to be sewn to the bag (see Sewing leather handles, page 21). Plastic hoop handles are also available in many colours and effects, or you could use natural bamboo. Other bags use fabric straps made from the fat quarter fabrics (see Straps, handles and professional touches, page 19). Webbing can be substituted for these fabric straps if you prefer. It is also used to make the straps for the Pick and Mix Backpack.

Zips

I've used an easy method to insert zips throughout the book, using the zip tape like a patchwork strip. Therefore, the total width of the zips used for the bags is important. Measured across the tape, this should be 1in (2.5cm). Zips sold for making patchwork bags, with metal teeth and fancy pulls, measure 1in (2.5cm) wide and are available in various lengths. Choose strong, good quality zips as bag zips are opened and closed often and need to be tough.

The Quilter's Suitcase, Mini Pochette and Pick and Mix Backpack, use long zips that you can make easily from a length of continuous zipper (nylon coil zipper) and zip pulls (size 3 is 1in (2.5cm) wide). Information on making or adapting zips can be found on page 16.

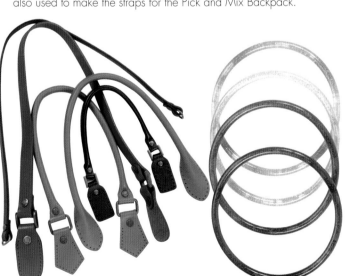

Techniques

This section describes the basics of rotary cutting, patchwork, quilting and bag making techniques used in this book. The specific patchwork method used for each pair of bags is included at the beginning of that chapter.

Rotary cutting

All the patchwork methods used in this book fall into two main groups – patchwork machine sewn with a ¼in (6mm) seam allowance (American patchwork) and patchwork machine sewn on to a foundation of calico and wadding (batting) (foundation piecing). Cut all the fabrics for these very efficiently using a rotary cutter, ruler and cutting mat.

A standard ¼in (6mm) seam allowance all round is added to all patchwork pieces when cutting out and you can sew this allowance accurately with the quarter inch foot on your sewing machine for accurate patchwork without templates.

Cutting fabric pieces

With the ruler firmly on top of your fabric, square off uneven ends of the fabric before you start and cut off the tightly woven selvage. Cut with the grain of the fabric (with printed stripes and checks, cut with the pattern). Turn your cutting mat through 180 degrees and line up the relevant mark on the ruler – for example, 2½in (6.5cm) if 2in (5cm) is the finished size. Line up your rotary cutter against the ruler's edge and cut (see photo 1).

Cut the larger pieces you need for each project first (see photo 2), as the smaller pieces can be cut from the remainder of the fat quarter – the individual bag instructions tell you when and what size to cut as you make each bag.

You can cut strips very economically to standard sizes for squares and rectangles, such as 2½in (6.5cm) squares and 1½in x 2½in (4cm x 6.5cm) rectangles from the same 2½in (6.5cm) strip (see photo 3). The bias binding is also cut from one of the fat quarters (see Making bias binding, page 18).

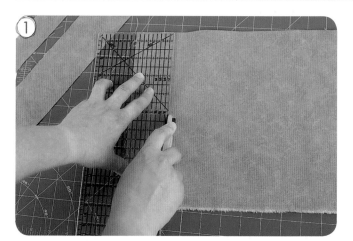

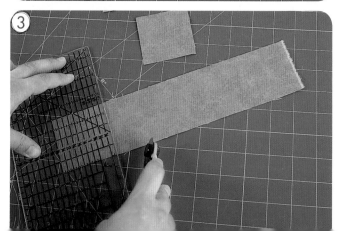

Machine piecing patchwork (American patchwork)

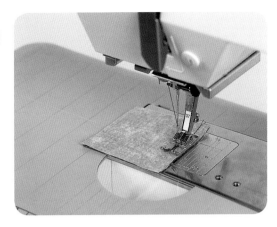

This method is used for the Typo Satchel, the Swag Bag and the Quilter's Suitcase chapters. Place your first two pieces right sides together, making sure the edges to be sewn line up. Set your sewing machine to a slightly shorter than average stitch length and check the tension is even. Use the quarter inch foot and line up the fabric edge with the edge of the foot when you sew. It may help if you sit slightly to the right of the machine needle so that you can see this easily.

Chain piecing is an industrial technique that speeds up piecing patchwork. When you have sewn your first two pieces together, don't cut the thread. Place the next two pieces together and sew them a stitch or two after the first two. Continue to make a 'chain', which can be cut up afterwards. When chain piecing strips, pin them together in pairs and hold the end of the strips under slight tension as they are fed through the machine, so the ends match up neatly.

TIP

If your machine tends to loop up the first few stitches, use a piece of scrap fabric as a 'leader' when you begin and chain piece the first two patchwork pieces on to that.

Foundation piecing

Simple foundation piecing is an easy patchwork method, dealt with in more detail in the relevant bag chapters. If the foundation includes wadding (batting), the patchwork is quilted as it is made and any further quilting is optional. The Strippy Handbag has no extra quilting while the Pick and Mix Backpack has extra crosshatched quilting over the top. The foundation fabric is cut to the required size and pinned to a slightly larger piece of wadding (batting) (photo 1). This panel is turned over so the wadding is on the top, replacing the pins so they can be removed as you sew.

A series of fabric strips are cut, following the instructions. Place the first piece face up on the foundation panel as directed (photo 2). Place the second piece face down on the first piece, pin and machine sew the two pieces together with a ¼in (6mm) seam along the long edge only, through the foundation (photo 3). Flip the second piece over so the right side is showing and finger press firmly. Continue adding pieces in this way until the foundation strip is covered.

The Eclipse Bag uses an appliqué version of this technique while the Laptop Bag has an extra calico layer, marked with lines, to help create the patchwork pattern.

Pressing patchwork

Press each stage of your patchwork as you go along, with the seam allowance to one side, as later this will help stop the wadding (batting) from 'bearding' or coming through the seam. For American patchwork, press towards the darker fabric as pressing dark towards light can cause a shadow effect on paler fabrics. Pressing in alternate directions makes the seams interlock neatly when the work is assembled and avoids lumpy seams where four layers of the seam allowance meet. Press with a dry iron or just a little steam using an up and down action so that the patchwork is not stretched and distorted – you are pressing, not ironing!

Finger press foundation pieced patchwork, as ironing will squash down the wadding (batting) or even melt blended cotton/polyester wadding. With your patchwork on a firm surface, run your finger firmly along the seam, pressing it open. This method can also be used to press American patchwork as each seam is sewn, pressing with an iron when complete.

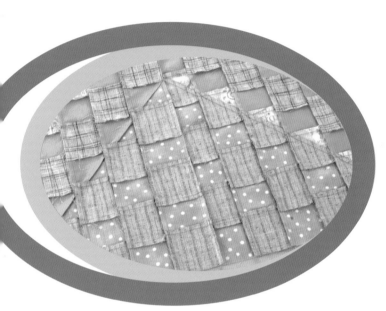

Making the quilt sandwich

American pieced patchwork is layered with backing fabric and wadding (batting) before quilting. Press the patchwork and backing fabric. Place the backing right side down on a flat surface, using masking tape to hold larger panels in place. Lay the wadding (batting) on top and smooth it out. Place the patchwork on top, making sure there is wadding and backing behind all the patchwork. Use your cutting mat and a quilter's ruler to check that the patchwork panel is square and not distorted. Pin or tack (baste) the three layers together. Pin with long quilting pins or curved safety pins, about 3in (7.5cm) apart, but take care when machine quilting near pins and remove them as you go. To tack, work from the centre outwards in a radiating pattern. Either method is suitable for the small pieces of quilting used in bags.

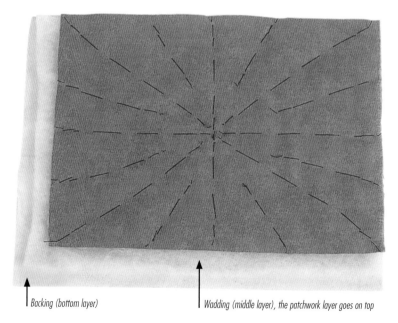

Backing (bottom layer)

Wadding (middle layer), the patchwork layer goes on top

Machine quilting with walking foot

Machine quilting gives a distinct line that can be used to emphasize the patchwork by quilting 'in the ditch' or along the patchwork seam line, on the other side of the seam from the patchwork seam allowance, or to add another simple pattern on top of the patchwork. If your machine has embroidery or interesting utility stitches, try with these for quilting. Set the machine to the 'needle down' position before you start quilting, so it will stop with the needle in the fabric. Some machines have a half speed feature that slows the stitching down, which you may find useful.

With the machine's feed dogs set 'up' and the walking foot, you can easily quilt in straight or gently curved lines. Working from the top, the walking foot helps to evenly feed all the layers through the machine at the same rate, working in unison with the feed dogs. Unlike quilting a large quilt, which should begin in the centre, starting and finishing at the edge of a small patchwork means there are fewer loose ends to finish off. Make sure the needle is down in the fabric before raising the presser foot to turn corners.

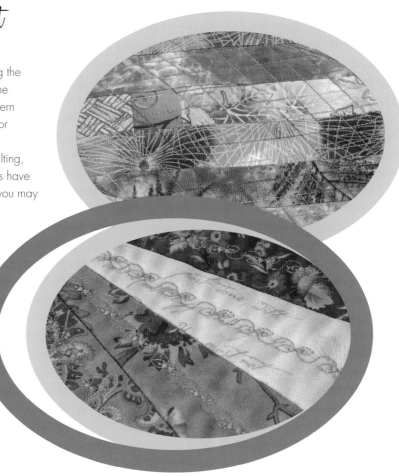

Trimming the bag panels

Trim each panel to the correct size before proceeding to assemble the bag, using your rotary cutting equipment for straight edges and scissors for curves. Machine around each panel first, about 1/8in (3mm) from the edge. Zigzagging or overlocking the edges of the panels after trimming will compress the wadding (batting) slightly, making bag assembly easier and preventing fraying.

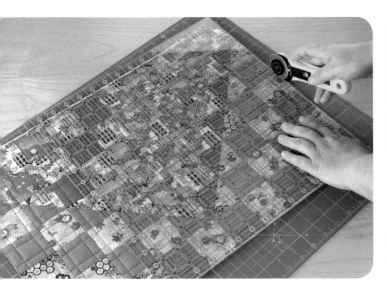

Making zips from nylon coil zipper

The zips used for the Quilter's Suitcase, Mini Pochette and Pick and Mix Backpack were all made from continuous nylon coil zipper, the kind sold for upholstery. This is a very inexpensive way to make zips and you can make them exactly the length you need. There is no need to crimp the end with metal, because the ends of the zip will be encased in a bag seam each time.

1 Start by taking hold of the end of the zip tape and gently pulling apart, as shown.

2 Making sure the outer part of the zip is on top, thread one zip pull on to one side of the tape. It will slide on quite easily. Move the zip pull so it is just hanging on to the end of the tape.

3 Thread the zip pull on to the other side of the tape. It is slightly harder to thread the second side of the tape than the first, because the zip teeth will start to engage through the pull. You might need a friend to help you by holding the tape taut. The ends of the zip tape are almost invariably slightly staggered. Rather than trying to align them perfectly each time, simply trim them to the same length. Be careful not to slide the zip pull off the tape as you open and close the zip while sewing it to the fabric. Cut the zip to the required length.

4 Make double pull zips that open in either direction by threading a zip pull from either end of the zip tape. You may need several attempts to get both sides of the zip tape lining up where the pulls meet.

5 If you can get different styles of pull for your continuous zip tape, consider using several different styles on one project, such as the Pick and Mix Backpack. Pulls with a loop can have ribbon added and are suitable where the zip needs to be flat and unobtrusive, like the hidden pocket in the back of the backpack, while pulls with a bar or bobble are easy to hold.

Inserting zips

Zips are used for several bags, including the Swag Bag and the Strippy Handbag. They are inserted using variations on the same basic method, where the zip is sewn between the outer panel and the bag lining, as if it is part of the patchwork. This is dealt with in more detail where relevant in each chapter. The basic method is shown here, using the gusset strip for the Swag Bag.

1   First, pin the outer fabric to the zip, carefully lining up the edge of the panel with one edge of the zip tape.

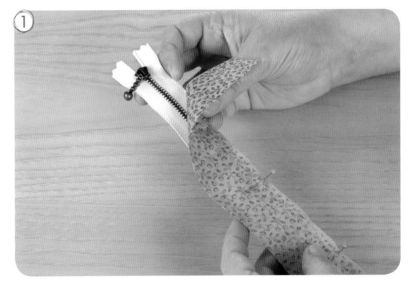

2   Turn the zip over and pin the matching lining panel to the other side of the zip. Tack (baste) the outer panel and lining to the zip to hold them together more accurately for sewing, if you wish. Sew the zip between the outer panel and lining using the zipper foot, stitching ¼in (6mm) from the edge – you may be able to stitch this using the quarter inch foot on your machine, but the left of the foot will run along the top of the zip teeth and you will need to prevent it slipping off the teeth as you sew. When you come to the part of the zip with the zip pull, stop sewing with the needle down, raise the presser foot and slide the zip pull beyond the area you are stitching, before lowering the foot and continuing to the end of the seam.

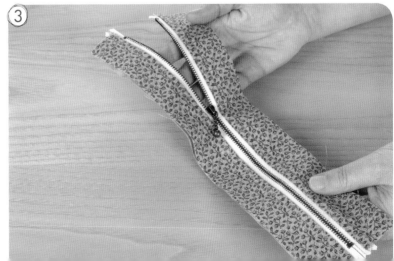

3   Finger press the outer panel and lining away from the zip teeth. Repeat the steps above to sew the other outer panel and lining section to the opposite side of the zip tape. Finish the zip strip by topstitching though the panel, zip tape and lining, approximately ⅛in (3mm) from the edge of the fabric closest to the zip teeth.

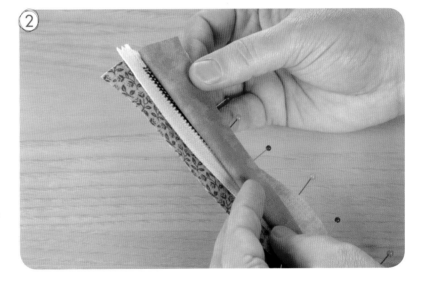

Making bias binding

Most of the bags in this book have their seams finished on the outside with bias binding, a construction method that helps to give the bags a good, firm shape without the need for rigid interfacings. Each bag chapter gives suggestions on which fabric to select for bias binding strips from your fat quarter assortment – 1¼in (3.2cm) is an adequate width for single bias binding, covering the bulk of the seam. There is no need to press any folds before sewing the binding to your bag.

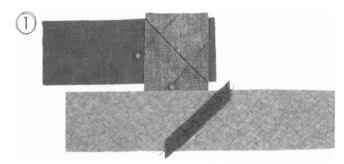

TIP

Get the most from your binding fabric by using the rest in the patchwork. Once you have cut enough strips to make the binding, sew the two leftover large triangles together along the bias edge. You can continue to use this panel to cut more bag pieces, such as pocket linings for the Laptop Bag, across the seam.

1 Cut 1¼in (3.2cm) wide bias strips for single bias binding or 2in (5cm) wide strips for double bias binding, (see above), using the 45-degree angle on your quilters' ruler. The first few strips will be around 24in (61cm) long, but subsequent strips will be shorter. Cut the ends on a 45-degree angle (they will be almost on this angle when first cut) and join strips together, pressing the seams open.

2 Pin the binding to the edge of the patchwork panel, matching the binding's raw edge to the bag edge, as described in the individual bag project. For double bias binding, you will be pinning through two layers of binding. Take care not to stretch bias binding when easing around corners. Machine sew the binding in place, following the instructions for each bag.

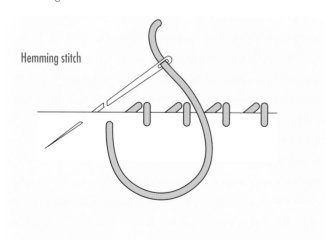

3 Turn the binding to the back, folding it snugly around the patchwork edge. Turn under the raw edge of the bias binding. Stitch down the binding using blind hemming stitch, covering the previous sewing stitches and taking care not to twist the binding.

Hemming stitch

Straps, handles and professional touches

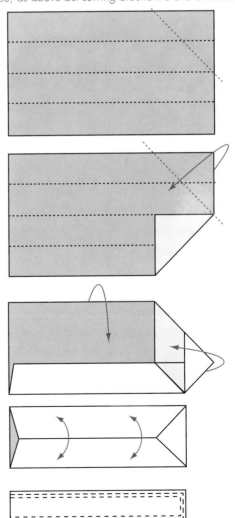

Bags like the Strippy Handbag and the Typo Satchel use a simple method for making straps from one of the fat quarter fabrics, while the Quilter's Suitcase and the Laptop Bag use ready-made leather handles, now sold by many quilt shops.

For fabric straps, cut the strips parallel to the selvedge, as the fabric is less stretchy along the warp than across the width. You will need to join strips together to obtain longer lengths. As there will be four layers of fabric in each strap, join strips with a 45-degree angle to reduce bulk. The long sides are folded into the centre of the strip, then folded in half lengthwise again for both open and closed ends. Press the fold at each stage. Cutting sizes are given with each bag. Shoulder bags with narrow straps will benefit from an additional strap pad (see page 20).

Making an open end strap

Use this method where the ends of the strap will be sewn into a seam, such as the Strippy Handbag (page 24). Following Fig A, fold and press the strip in half lengthwise. Open it out. Fold and press the sides to meet the centre crease. Fold the folded sides to the centre, so there are four layers of fabric. Pin and sew along the strip several times, with the first line of stitching about $1/16$ in (1 mm) from the edge. A strip of wadding, slightly narrower than the finished strap width, can be folded into the strap after the sides are pressed, enclosing it under one of the first side folds, but will make adding eyelets more difficult due to increased thickness.

Making a closed end strap

Eyelet straps, as on the Typo Satchel, need neat ends. Start by making the same folds as for the open end strap. Following Fig B, fold over the end corners on a 45-degree angle along the red dashes and press. Fold the sides and end in, creating a mitred arrangement at one end. Fold the strip in half, pin and sew along the strip twice, as above but sewing around the end of the strip.

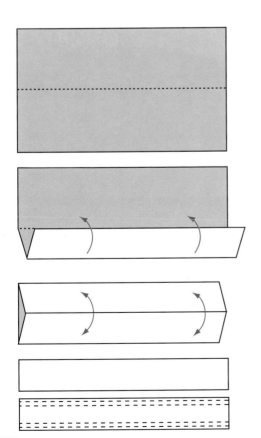

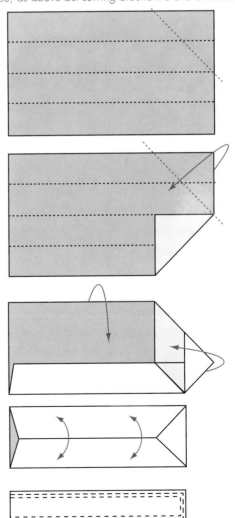

Fig A

Fig B

Making a strap pad

Using two 8½in x 2½in (21.6cm x 6.4cm) rectangles of fabric and a rectangle of wadding (batting) approximately the same size, curve the ends of each rectangle with a circle template, as shown in Fig C. Cut the fabric you want to have on the top of the pad in half lengthwise, along the dashed line. Pin the wider piece to the wadding right side up and pin the piece you cut lengthwise on top, right side down i.e. right sides together. Machine sew the layers together, ¼in (6mm) from the edge. Trim the wadding (batting) back to the stitching line and clip around the curves.

Turn the pad right side out through the gap, as shown by the red arrows. Press the edge and top stitch around the pad close to the edge if you wish. Tack (baste) the raw edges on the top of the pad and pin the pad *under* the strap when you machine sew the strap, so the raw edges are hidden by the strap. You can herringbone stitch the raw edges together by hand if you prefer, leaving the stitches in place.

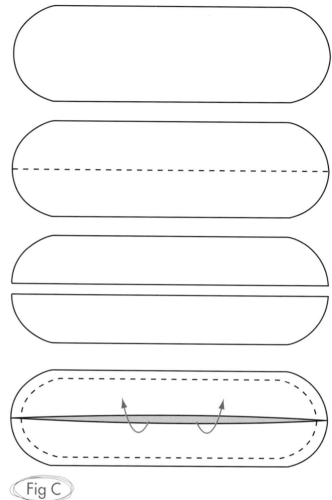

Herringbone stitch

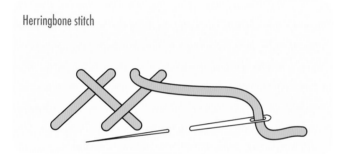

Fig C

Adding buckles and eyelets

When buying buckles, check that the inner measurement will fit your bag strap. The Typo Satchel and the Pick and Mix Backpack all use buckles for 1in (2.5cm) wide straps. If you cannot find the correct buckle size, cloth straps can be widened slightly to fit (cut strips four times the width of the finished strap). Webbing must be the right size for slide release buckles or tri-glide slide buckles. Slip buckles on to their straps before the strap is folded over and sewn to the bag. Make a hole for the prong where necessary using a bodkin or stiletto, pushing the fabric fibres apart rather than cutting them, which could fray later. Some pronged buckles tend to slip back off the fold, so hold them in place by hand stitching several times through all the layers just behind the buckle prong.

Eyelets need to be 'set', crimped in place using eyelet pliers or a setting tool, following the manufacturer's instructions. You will need to punch a hole first. Practice on a scrap, folding the fabric so you are punching and setting the eyelet through the same number of fabric layers as your strap.

Sewing leather handles

Ready-made leather handles have holes to stitch through, so you do not need a leather needle to sew them to your bag. A large crewel needle or similar will do, with 'jeans' thread, buttonhole thread or hand quilting thread (doubled). Waxing the thread will make sewing easier. Use a small piece of double-sided sticky tape to temporarily hold the strap in place while you sew.

Starting with a knot on the back of the bag panel and a couple of stitches through the first holes, backstitch around the end of the strap, taking care to stitch through the ready-made holes. Finish with two stitches through the last pair of holes and fasten off securely on the back of the work. Bags with leather handles cannot be completely immersed in water, so if you want to pop your bag in the washing machine, you will have to add the leather straps when the bag is finished, stitching through the lining, and remove them for washing – or use fabric straps instead.

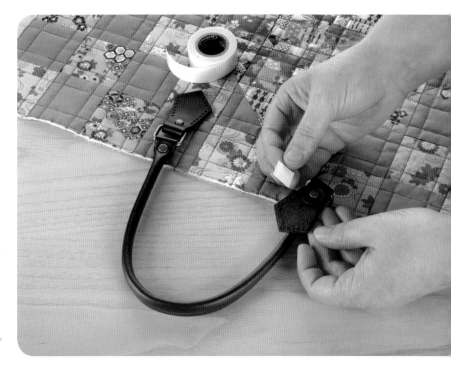

Adapting bags

As shown in all of the bag chapters, the simplest way to change a bag is by using a different fat quarter selection and this will suggest new themes for trims and embellishments too. Where trace-off patterns are given, you can resize them on a photocopier, but remember that other pieces, such as bag gussets, will also need to be resized. Measuring around the bag panel, ¼in (6mm) from the panel edge, using a tape measure standing up on edge so you can go around curves, is a good way to check that your adaptations are going to fit together. Whatever fat quarters you choose, you can bet your bag will be unique!

The Projects

Strippy Handbag
and Wedge Purse

Start Monday off in casual style to ease you into the week with this handbag and purse in African cottons, ideal accessories when you're catching up with friends after the weekend. Just two fabrics are packed with colour and pattern variations, so they give the illusion of many more ultra coordinated materials. Can you believe that there's only one fabric on the bag side panels?

The easy stitch and flip strip patchwork, pieced and quilted in one, is great for really big, bold designs. Cutting strips across stripes on the other fat quarter makes the patchwork look more intricate on the bag gusset too. The folded fabric strap is attached while the gusset is pieced. Circle motifs cut freehand from the second fabric make neat, raw edge appliqués on one side of the bag. A zip closure keeps your handbag secure.

Monday's little project

The matching wedge-shaped purse, also constructed with a gusset, sits neatly in the bag.

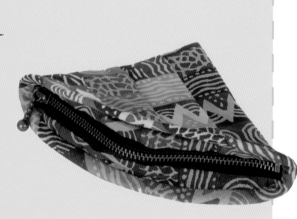

24

Patchwork method: Foundation piecing and raw edge appliqué

Sewing patchwork on to a foundation helps to stabilize it as you sew. By adding a layer of wadding (batting) on top of the calico foundation and sewing the patchwork through wadding and backing in one, your patchwork is quilted as it is sewn and no extra quilting is necessary unless decorative quilting is preferred.

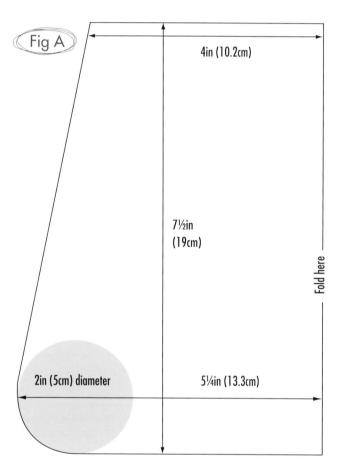

Fig A

4in (10.2cm)

7½in (19cm)

Fold here

2in (5cm) diameter

5¼in (13.3cm)

FABRIC IDEA

When you use just two fabrics, choose ones that 'work hard' by offering lots of pattern variation, or the patchwork pattern will be camouflaged in the print.

1   Using Fig A, draft the bag side panel pattern. Fold a piece of tracing paper in half before you begin, this is the fold line in the diagram. Draw one half of the diagram and flip the tracing paper over to trace the outline on to the other side of the fold. Open out the paper and cut out the template. Use it to cut two side panels from 8in x 10½in (20.3cm x 26.7cm) pieces of calico. Pin one calico side panel to the wadding (batting) and use it as a template to rotary cut the straight edges. Cut the corner curves with scissors.

2 Turn the panel over so the wadding is on top. Pin the wadding to the backing from the top so pins are visible and remove pins from the underside. Cut seven 1½in (3.8cm) wide strips across the width of one patchwork fabric. Using the foundation panel as a guide, cut the first strip so it overlaps the ends of the top of the panel. Pin the strip to the panel right side up, lining up the edge of the strip with the edge of the panel. Machine sew ⅛in (3mm) from the edge.

TIP

A walking foot will feed through all the layers in foundation piecing without rucking up or puckering. Most walking feet have a quarter inch mark on the foot, so align that with the edge of the patchwork strips.

3 Cut the next strip so it slightly overlaps the end of the foundation panel (arrange the patchwork strips for the most variety so the strips are more obvious). Keep the remaining, longer part of the strip to use further down the patchwork panel, where the sides flare out. Place it face down on the first strip, right sides together and pin. Machine sew patchwork, through both strips and the foundation, using ¼in (6mm) seam.

4 Flip over the second strip and finger press open, running your finger firmly along the seam. Pin the second strip down to hold it in place. Continue adding more strips the same way, until the whole panel is covered, using the leftover fabric from the first three strips for the last three, which are slightly longer (use the leftover from the centre strip from the first panel for the second centre strip). Turn the panel over and machine stitch around the edge, about ⅛in (3mm) from the edge. Trim the overhanging strips to match the backing panel, using your ruler and rotary cutter as you did in step 1. Make another panel.

5 Cut out motifs from your second fabric for the raw edge appliqué on one side panel. There is no need to add a turning allowance but cut slightly outside the motif outline. Arrange and pin the motifs to the bag panel. If you are going to sew leather handles to the bag panels, as for the rainbow batik version shown here, place a handle in roughly the right position, so you don't overlap an appliqué with the handle end. Using straight stitch and the standard machine foot (or an appliqué foot, if you have one), machine around each motif several times in matching thread. It doesn't matter if the stitch lines cross each other and the panel is firm enough not to need any tear-away stabiliser underneath. Pull thread ends through to the back and tie together to finish.

Monday's Projects

You Will Need

- Two fat quarters
- Plain calico backing and wadding (batting):
  - one 24in x 3in (60.9cm x 7.6 cm) piece for bag gusset
  - two 8in x 10½in (20.3cm x 26.7cm) pieces for bag side panels
  - one 9½in x 4¾in (24.1cm x 12cm) piece for purse panel
- Cotton quilting fabric for lining:
  - one 24in x 3in (60.9cm x 7.6 cm) piece for bag gusset
  - two 8in x 10½in (20.3cm x 26.7cm) pieces for bag side panels
  - one 9½in x 4¾in (24.1cm x 12cm) piece for purse panel
  - one 2½in x 7in (6.4cm x 17.8cm) piece for purse gusset

- One 17½in x 1in (44.5cm x 2.5cm) strip of wadding (batting) for bag handle
- 70in x 1¼in (177.8cm x 3.2cm) wide bias binding (see Making bias binding, page 18)
- One 7in (18cm) zip for bag – zip tape length is 8in (20.3cm)
- One 6¼in (16cm) zip for purse – zip tape length is 6¾in (17.1cm)
- Tracing paper
- Sewing threads to tone with patchwork

Strippy Handbag

Making the side panels

1 Make a paper pattern from Fig A on page 26 and cut out two side panels from the 8in x 10½in (20.3cm x 26.7cm) pieces of calico. Cut seven 1½in (3.8cm) wide strips across the width of one patchwork fabric. Make two side panels, as described on page 27. Out of your two fabrics, reserve the one with more suitable motifs for appliqué for the gusset panel, so your appliqué pieces will contrast sufficiently with the side panel patchwork strips. I cut small circular motifs from the second fabric and arranged these randomly for the raw edge appliqué on one side panel. Zigzag or overlock around each side panel.

2 A sashing strip across the top of the side panels makes inserting the zip easy, as there is no bulk. Cut two 8in x 1in (20.3cm x 2.54cm) strips from the side panel fabric. Right sides together, pin one strip across the top of the first bag panel, as shown. Machine sew the strip to the panel, using ¼in (6mm) seam. Press the seam towards the strip. Repeat for the other panel. Using each completed side panel as a pattern, cut lining panels from the two 8in x 10½in (20.3cm x 26.7cm) lining pieces.

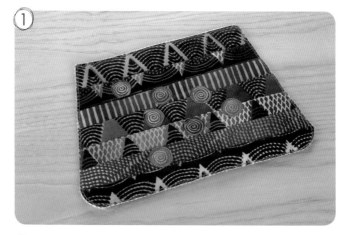

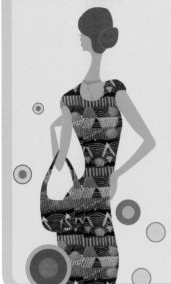

FABRIC IDEA

Both fabrics had motifs arranged in rows, in patterned stripes with multicoloured shading. The fabric with the wider stripes had pattern contrast between strips when cut along the pattern. The narrow bands of the second fabric suggested cutting across, so the patchwork would seem more elaborate. You can cut the patchwork strips in either direction for maximum variety.

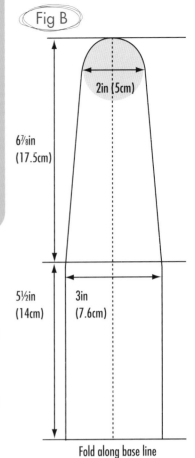

Fig B

2in (5cm)

6⅞in (17.5cm)

5½in (14cm)

3in (7.6cm)

Fold along base line

Making the handle and bag gusset

3 Following Fig B, draft a pattern for the gusset foundation using tracing paper. As with drafting the pattern from Fig A (page 26), if you begin by folding the tracing paper along the base line of the pattern, you can draft one half of the pattern using a quilting ruler and 2in (5cm) circle template, then trace it on to the other half of the folded paper. Open it out for a complete pattern. Make a bag gusset foundation using the 24in x 3in (60.9m x 7.6 cm) backing and wadding (batting) pieces, as for the side panels. Turn it over so the wadding is on the top and the pins are visible.

4 Cut one 4in (10.2cm) wide strip down the *side* of the second fat quarter, parallel to the selvedge, for your bag handle. If you are using an imperial fat quarter this will measure a nominal 18in (45.7cm) long. Metric fat quarters will be slightly longer, approximately 19⅝in (50cm) long, so you would need to trim to 18in (45.7cm). Choose a section of the pattern that will make an interesting design when folded, like the zigzag design shown here. Make an open end strap, following the instructions on page 19, using the 17½ x 1in (44.5cm x 2.5cm) strip of wadding (batting) to pad the handle. Cut several 1¼in (3.2cm) bias strips from the remainder of the fat quarter and join them to make one 70in (177.8cm) strip for bias binding, enough to bind the purse, too (see Making bias binding, page 18).

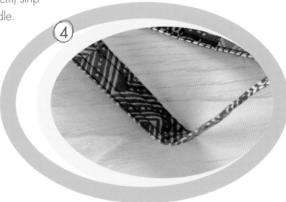

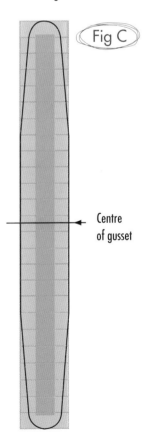

Fig C

Centre of gusset

5 Mark the centre of the gusset foundation with a pin at either side, as shown in Fig C. Cut twenty-five 3in x 1½in strips from the second fabric. Begin by pinning a strip across the centre. Pin and machine sew a second strip to one side and sew a third strip to the opposite side. Work outwards towards each end of the gusset, sewing more strips on to the foundation patchwork.

6 When you are within *two* strips of each end, pin the handle to the gusset. Note that the handle is shorter than the gusset panel, so you will not be able to lay the panel flat once the handle is pinned in place. Centre the handle on the gusset with the ends of the handle overlapping the edge of the last patchwork strip you sewed by 1in (2.5cm). The handle will be sewn to the gusset in each of the next two patchwork seams. Pin in place. Pin and machine sew the last two patchwork strips to the bag gusset. Trim the panel as described in step 4 on page 27. Use the gusset as a pattern to cut the lining, pinning the gusset to the 24in x 3in (60.9cm x 7.6cm) piece of lining fabric, wrong sides together. Trim the lining to match and machine sew all round, about ⅛in (3mm) from the edge. Machine overlock or zigzag the raw edges.

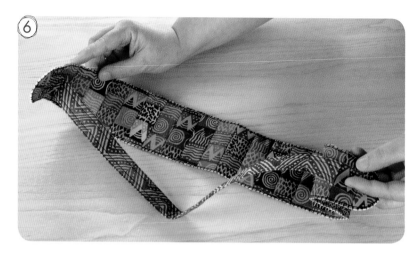

Inserting the zip

7 With the 7in (18cm) zip right side down against the top of the bag panel, line up the edge of the panel with one edge of the zip tape and pin together, as shown. The zip tape needs to extend all the way along the top of the panel but the teeth must stop more than ¼in (6mm) from each end, to allow for assembling the bag.

8 Right sides together, pin one of the lining panels (cut out in step 2, page 27) to the bag panel, sandwiching the zip in between. Tack (baste) the outer panel and lining to the zip to hold them together more accurately for sewing, if you wish. Sew the zip between the outer panel and lining using the zipper foot, stitching ¼in (6mm) from the edge, following the instructions on page 17.

9 Repeat steps 7 and 8 to sew the zip to the other side panel. Once complete, check the zip opens correctly. Pin the lining fabric to the back of each side panel and machine stitch around the panel, ⅛in (3mm) from the edge. Machine overlock or zigzag the raw edges.

Completing the bag

10 Find the centre along the bottom edges of the finished bag panel and gusset by folding each in half and marking the centre point with coloured pins. Linings together, align the centre pin on one side of the gusset with the centre pin on one side of the bag panel and start pinning the pieces together from this point, working along the bottom of the bag, lining up the outside edges. Pin the sides of the gusset to the sides of the bag panels, lining up the centre of the each end of the gusset with the centre of the zip. Clip around the straight sections to go around the curves at the corners of the bag panels and each end of the gusset strip, clipping about 1/8 in (3mm) in from the panel edge, so you can ease one section to the other at these points. Machine sew the gusset to the bag panel.

11 Sew bias binding to finish off the raw edges. Pin the bias binding to the outside of the bag, leaving enough binding to join the ends at a 45-degree angle on a straight section (along the bag side is ideal). Ease the bias binding around the curved bottom corners and around the top of the gusset. Turn the work over and machine sew with the binding underneath so you can line your stitches up on top of the previous stitching, exactly 1/4 in (6mm) from the edge. Turn under the binding so it is a snug fit to the edge and slipstitch all round.

TIP

Machine sewing around three-dimensional curves is easier if you sew the seam in stages. Sew around the curve at the top of the gusset with the curved piece at the bottom, starting and finishing on a straight section. Turn the bag over to sew around the bottom corners.

Over the rainbow

If a quick trip to the supermarket is on your list, you'll feel more upbeat with bright, rainbow-dyed batiks, another range of fabrics that have a lot of colour and pattern variation in one print. Both these batiks include a rainbow of colour. The addition of the strong black leaf outlines on the second fabric makes the colours seem even more intense and glowing. The leaves were ideal for the raw edge appliqué, lending themselves to a natural arrangement on the bag panel. I changed the fabric strap for the leather handles sewn to the side panels, so it feels like a different bag.

Wedge Purse

Making the panel

1 Make a paper pattern from Fig C, folding the paper
as indicated, and cut out one side panel from the one
9½in x 4¾in (24cm x 12cm) piece of calico. Cut four 1½in
(3.8cm) wide strips, two 9½in (24cm), one 8½in (21.6cm)
and one 7½in (19cm) long. I used the same fabric for the purse
patchwork as for the bag side panels. Make one panel, starting
with one of the longest strips lined up along the straight edge,
as described on page 27. Zigzag or overlock around the panel.

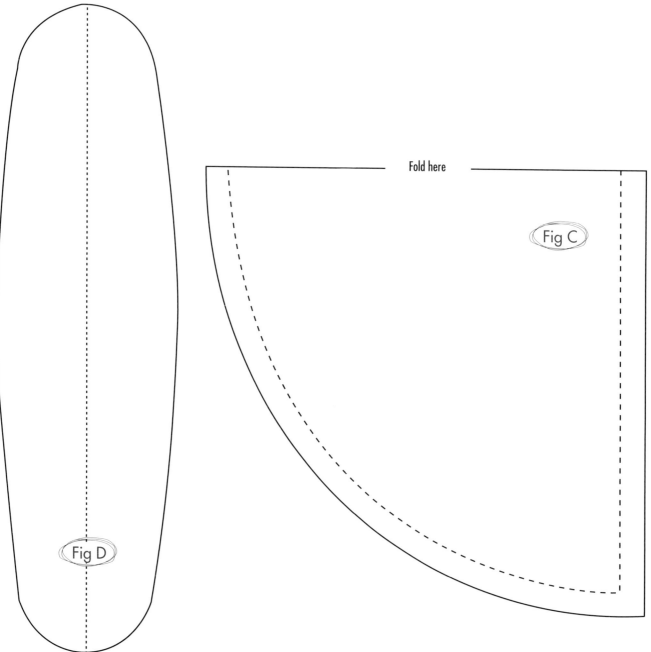

Fig D

Fold here

Fig C

Making the zip gusset

2 Using the pattern piece in Fig D, cut one gusset from the second patchwork fabric and one from the remaining lining piece. Cut each piece in half, along the dotted line marked in the diagram. Use these strips to make a zip gusset, following the instructions for inserting zips on page 17. First, pin one half of the gusset strip to one side of the zip, right sides together.

3 Turn the zip over and pin the right side of the lining to the back of zip. Machine sew.

4 Repeat with the other pieces of gusset and lining to complete the zip gusset, as shown. Press the fabric strips away from the zip. Machine sew the outer fabric to the lining around the gusset panel, ⅛in (3mm) from the edge.

Completing the purse

5 Using the patchwork panel as a pattern, cut the purse lining from the 9½ x 4¾in (24cm x 12cm) piece of lining fabric. The purse lining and purse seam are sewn in one step. Fold the purse in half and fold the lining in half, right sides together. Place the folded lining on top of the folded purse, as shown, and pin. Machine sew along the straight side.

6 Put your hand inside the layers, taking hold of the outer panel, and gently pull it out towards you, as shown. Turn the purse right side out, by folding the outer panel back over the lining.

7 Use a point turner to make sure the corner of the purse is well turned out. Line up the edge of the lining with the edge of the purse, pin and machine sew all round, ⅛in (3mm) from the edge.

8 Using coloured pins to mark the midpoint of the purse curve, line up the gusset with the purse so the seam will be on the outside. One end of the zip will line up with the purse panel seam and the other with the midpoint pin. Machine sew the gusset to the purse, clipping about ⅛in (3mm) in from the purse edge, so you can ease the purse around the curved ends of the gusset, working in two stages if necessary (see Strippy Handbag step 10, page 31). Finish by binding the seam with bias binding (see page 18 and step 11, page 31).

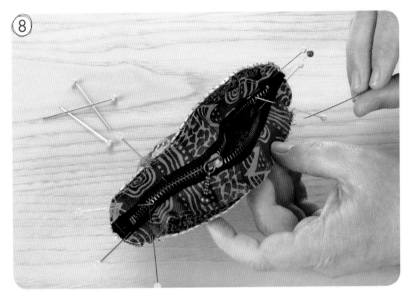

TIP

If machine sewing around the fairly tight curves at each end of the purse is difficult for you, backstitch the gusset into the purse instead.

FABRIC IDEA

Two fabrics inspired by vintage kimono silks would work well together for these bags, giving a hint of Japanese Taisho-era style. One has large rectangles of complimentary geometrics and large-scale patterns, which would give a lot of variety for the side panels. The other has a busier design on a slightly smaller scale.

Eclipse Bag
and Celestial Circles Purse

Tuesday's special night out is complemented with a galaxy of stars in appliqué circles for my evening bag and purse. These metallic prints with celestial designs include similar shades of blue, but the patterns have plenty of contrast in scale and tone. That extra sparkle is emphasized with metallic organza layers between the appliqué layers, like the sun's corona in an eclipse, although here it is also visible in the cut out central circle.

Even the appliqué thread is sparkly, edging each circle with machine blanket stitch. The appliqué is sewn on to a wadding (batting) and backing foundation, so the quilting is done at the same time. Glittery transparent hoop handles continue the circular theme. The ruched gusset is gathered with two drawstrings, which can be drawn up to alter the shape of the bag.

Tuesday's little project

The coin purse is very easy to make and echoes the evening bag with circle appliqués on a smaller scale. You can enjoy feeling like the star for the night!

Appliqué method: Raw edge appliqué on foundation

Sewing appliqué on to a foundation helps stabilize it as you sew and you don't need to do any extra quilting. A layer of wadding (batting) is sandwiched underneath the appliqué background fabric and on top of the calico foundation.

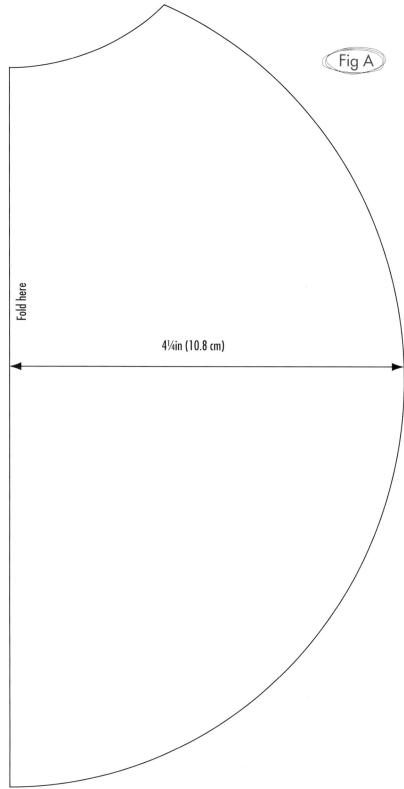

Fig A

Fold here

4¼in (10.8 cm)

FABRIC IDEA

A good contrast in value, pattern and scale will prevent the fabrics merging into one another and keep the appliqué shapes distinct.

1 Using Fig A, trace a paper template. Fold the paper in half before you begin and line up the fold on the fold line in the diagram. Trace the diagram and flip the tracing paper over to trace the outline on to the other side of the fold. Open out the paper and cut out the template. Use it to cut two side panels from the first fat quarter – choose the fabric you want to use for the background. Place one 9in (22.9cm) diameter wadding (batting) circle on top of one of the calico circles and place one side panel piece on top of that. Smooth out the fabrics and wadding and pin through all the layers.

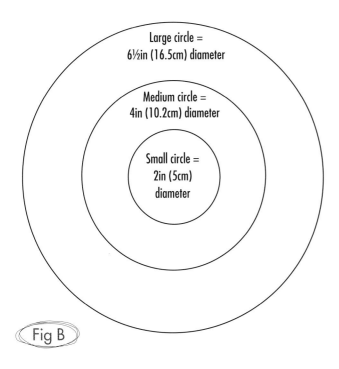

Large circle =
6½in (16.5cm) diameter

Medium circle =
4in (10.2cm) diameter

Small circle =
2in (5cm)
diameter

Fig B

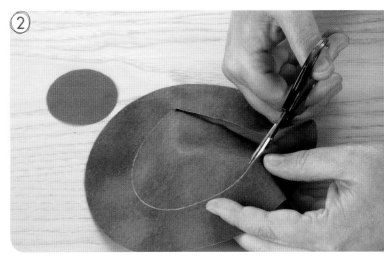

2 Using Fig B as a guide to template sizes, mark and cut out the circle appliqués. You can simply cut out three circles and overlap them or just use the outer and inner ones, as I have done here, so the background fabric shows through in the design.

3 Arrange and pin the circle appliqués on the background fabric, pinning securely through the wadding (batting) and backing layers, as shown. Centre the circles within the design, but make sure the outer circle is no closer then $^3/_8$ in (1cm) to the top edge of the bag (the shallow arc on the right in the photo), or the edge will be lost in the top seam when the bag is assembled.

TIP

Using a quilting needle to stitch the appliqué through the foundation and wadding (batting) reduces the risk of skipped stitches. Using a walking foot for the appliqué feeds all the wadding and fabric layers through at the same rate.

4 Machine sew around each circle in turn, using machine blanket stitch or another suitable edge stitch, gradually turning around the circle on the machine as you stitch. You could use raw edge appliqué (see page 27) if you prefer. Take care not to hit the pins as you sew. Machine sew around the panel, ⅛in (3mm) from the edge. Trim the wadding and backing to match the panel edge. Machine overlock or zigzag the edge.

Tuesday's Projects

You Will Need

- Three fat quarters
- Plain calico backing and wadding (batting):
  - two 9in (22.9cm) diameter circles for bag side panels
  - one 5in (12.7cm) diameter circle for purse side panels
- Cotton quilting fabric for lining:
  - two 9in (22.9cm) diameter circles for bag side panels
  - two 5in (12.7cm) diameter circles for purse side panels

- Four 5in (12.7cm) diameter circles of sparkly nylon organza (for starry colourway)
- 70in x 1¼in (177.8cm x 3.2cm) wide bias binding (see Making bias binding, page 18)
- Two 5in (13cm) plastic hoop handles for bag
- 70in (177.8cm) 'rat's tail' cord or other fine cord for bag drawstrings
- Two spring toggles for drawstrings (optional)
- One 4in (10.2cm) zip, for purse (zip tape length is 5in (12.7cm) approx.)
- Tracing paper

- Sewing and quilting threads to tone with patchwork
- Metallic machine embroidery thread (for starry colourway)

TIP
Change to a metallica needle to machine quilt with metallic embroidery thread. Loosen the top tension slightly and stitch slowly, so you don't fray and break the thread.

Eclipse Evening Bag

Making the side panels

1 Using Fig A and instructions in step 1 on page 38, make a paper template and cut out four side panel pieces from the same fabric. Keep two pieces for the bag lining. I used the darkest fabric in my fat quarter bundle. Prepare two side panels with foundation wadding (batting) and calico as described on page 38. Cut three 21in x 3½in (53.3cm x 8.9cm) strips for the gathered bag gusset across the width of the fat quarter fabric you want for the largest appliqué circle and keep to use in step 7.

Using Fig B on page 39, cut out two 6½in circles from the mid-toned fat quarter and two 4in circles from the lightest fabric. Cut out a 2in circle from the centre of each 4in circle. Following the instructions in steps 2–4 on page 39, layer the fabrics as shown, including two layers of organza circles underneath the central 'hoop' circle, one at right angles to the background fabric and one at 45-degrees. Machine sew. Make two identical side panels.

2 Tease out and fray the raw edge of the two organza layers on each side panel. Because one of the organza circles is on a 45-degree angle on each side, the thin frayed edge effect of just one layer is avoided and the threads will create a very soft, slightly irregular, sparkly halo around the circle.

Attaching the handles

3 Cut six 3in x 2½in (7.6cm x 6.4cm) strips from the background fabric. Following the instructions for making an open end strap on page 19, make six tab loops, 2½in x ¾in (6.4cm x 1.9cm). These loops attach the bag to the hoop handles. Pin one tab to the centre of the top of one panel, as shown, with the tab lying over the panel. Pin another tab on either side of the first one, positioning these tabs ½in (1.3cm) from the top corners of the panel. Tack (baste) in place.

4 Wrap each tab over the hoop handle, lining up the tab ends, pin and machine sew in place. Once the tabs are wrapped over the handle, it will be impossible to lay the top panel completely flat, but this does not make sewing the tabs very difficult. Use the narrower ¼in (6mm) foot rather than the walking foot to do this, as the latter will catch the side of the hoop handle as you sew.

5 Right sides together, with the hoop handle and tabs sandwiched in between, pin one lining panel (cut in step 1) to the top of the panel, as shown. Machine sew across the top of the panel.

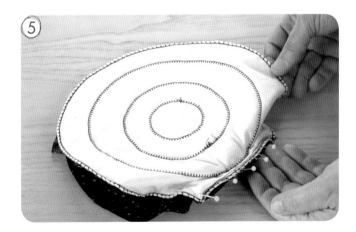

6 Flip the lining piece over and the hoop handle is attached to the top of the panel by the loops. Finger press the seam (don't use an iron in case you melt the handle!) and machine sew parallel to the panel top, ¼in (6mm) from the edge. Machine overlock or zigzag around the outer edge of the circular side panel, sewing the lining to the panel. Repeat steps 3–6 for the other side panel.

Making the bag gusset

7 Cut one of the 21in x 3½in (53.3cm x 8.9cm) strips from step 1 in half, to make two pieces 10½in (26.7cm) long. Sew one of the shorter strips to each of the longer ones, to make two strips 31in (78.7cm) long. Use ¼in (6mm) seam allowance and press seams open. Machine overlock or zigzag the short ends of the strips. Place the strips right sides together, arranging them so the short joining seams don't overlap, and pin together across the short ends. Machine sew the ends together with a ³/₈in (1cm) seam allowance, but leaving a ¾in (1.9cm) gap unsewn exactly in the centre of the seam, as shown, for the drawstring channels.

Press seam allowances open and machine sew them in position, stitching about ¼in (6mm) from the seam, to stop the drawstrings pulling the seam allowances out through the openings when you use the bag.

8 Line up the long sides of the gusset strip and its identical lining, now joined across the ends, and pin. Mark three lines along the gusset, as shown – one straight down the centre and the other two ³/₈in (1cm) on either side of the centre line. Machine sew straight down each line to complete the drawstring channels, starting and finishing with a few backstitches.

9 Loosen the machine's top tension to zero and, with the longest possible stitch length, sew a gathering thread along each side of the gusset, about ⅛in (3mm) from the edge, leaving the ends long enough to hold and gather. Place pins on either side of the gusset, at the centre. Line up the gusset with the first side panel, with the panel lining against the back of the gusset, lining up the pins along the centre edge of the patchwork, going around the curve. Gently pulling on the gathering thread that looks tightest, begin to gather up the gusset to match the edge of the side panel. Smooth out the gathers as you work, so they are nice and even. Hold them in place by pinning at right angles to the panel edge, with the pin heads on the outside, as shown, and fasten off the gathering threads by twisting in a figure of eight around the pins at each end.

10 Machine sew around the outside edge of the side panel, sewing through the gathered and lined gusset and the bag lining, keeping the gathers neat and removing each pin as you come to it. When finished, remove the gathering thread by pulling the tightest thread first – it will come out easily – undoing the gathering stitches so you can pull the remaining thread away.

11 Repeat steps 9 and 10 to gather and sew the gusset to the other side of the bag.

Completing the bag

12 Pin bias binding to the outside of the bag, leaving approx. ¾in (1.9cm) extra binding at each end. Ease the bias binding around the curve, without it stretching. Turn the work over and machine sew with the binding underneath, so you can line your stitches up on top of the previous stitching, exactly ¼in (6mm) from the edge. Fold in the ends of the binding at the top of the bag and stitch in place, then turn under the binding so it is a snug fit to the edge and slipstitch all round.

13 Cut the cord into two equal pieces for the drawstrings. Thread one piece through each channel. Thread both cords at one end through one spring toggle and repeat at the other end of the cord. The spring toggle will sit against the top of the gusset when the bag is used. Finish the ends of the cords with a padded bobble. Cut one 3½in (8.9cm) circle for each bobble, turn under a ¼in (6mm) hem and stitch a gathering thread all round. Tease some oddments of wadding (batting) or cotton wool into the middle of the bobble. Tie a knot in the end of the cord. Pull up the gathering thread, slipping the bobble over the knotted end of the cord and tighten the thread, adding a few stitches through the cord to hold the bobble in place.

Right on target

Keeping the same hoop handles but with target circles in red, white and blue, change the look to sixties 'mod' for some retro collectibles shopping downtown. Strong colour contrasts emphasize the circles and the machine stitched outlines are sharper without the raw edged organza. Rather than use all solid colours, plain red contrasts with blue metallic and a textured tone-on-tone white adds subtlety to the iconic graphic image. This time, the outer appliqué circle is cut as a hoop and the centre circle is appliquéd, rather than being reverse appliqué. The appliqué threads were matched as closely as possible to the fabrics.

Celestial Circles Purse

Making the side panels

1 Using Fig C as a guide, make a set of paper templates and cut out two 4½in (11.4cm) circles from your darkest fabric, one 3½in (8.9cm) circle from the medium tone fabric and one 2in (5cm) circle from the lightest fabric for your purse panels. Appliqué the circles, following instructions in step 1, page 40. Cut two more 4½in (11.4cm) circles from the medium tone fabric to use for the purse lining. Cut one 5in (12.7cm) diameter circle of wadding (batting) and backing fabric.

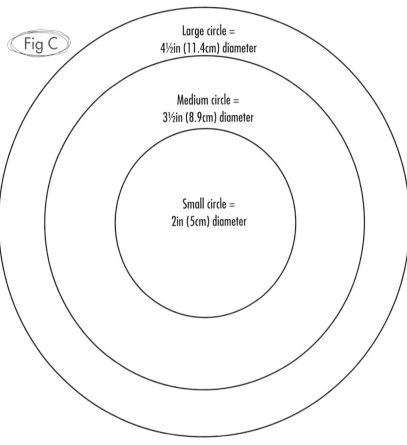

Fig C

Large circle = 4½in (11.4cm) diameter

Medium circle = 3½in (8.9cm) diameter

Small circle = 2in (5cm) diameter

2 Prepare one side panel with foundation wadding (batting) and calico as described on page 38. Layer the appliqué circles, pin and stitch, as described in steps 3 and 4 on page 39. Trim the edges of the wadding and backing to match the edge of the appliqué side panel. Pin the panel to one of the 4½in (11.4cm) lining circles, back to back, and machine sew all round. Machine overlock or zigzag the edge.

Inserting the zip

3 Fold the second 4½in (11.4cm) dark outer fabric circle in half and cut through the centre. Repeat with the lining circle. Following the instructions for inserting a zip (page 17), pin and sew the 4in (10.2cm) zip between one outer fabric and one lining semicircle. As the panels are only 4½in diameter and the zip is 4in (10.2cm) long, make sure the zip teeth begin and end ¼in (6mm) from the edge of the circle, so you don't hit the metal teeth with the machine needle later.

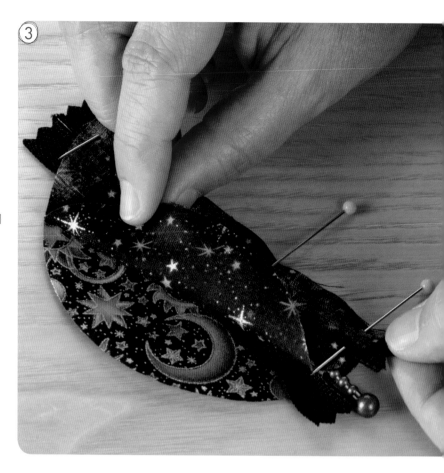

4 Sew the other semicircle of outer fabric and lining to the zip. Make sure both sides of the fabric match up. When finished, the circle will be joined back together by the zip, as shown. Trim the ends of the zip tape to match the sides of the circle to complete the zip panel.

Completing the purse

5 Place the appliqué side panel and the zip panel back to back, so the linings are together. Pin together and machine sew all round, ¼in (6mm) from the edge, taking care not to stitch over the metal at the ends of the zip. Finish by binding the outer edge with bias binding (see page 18 and page 44, step 12).

⑤

FABRIC IDEA

Go back to the future for a space odyssey with retro prints. The starburst motifs, which invite seed bead embellishments, are full of dynamic energy while the irregular circles and stripes provide a calming effect. Try a different colour for the hoop handles too.

Laptop Bag
and Gadget Pocket

Step out creatively on Wednesday with a funky briefcase-style bag – who would guess there's a laptop inside? I made mine to fit a smaller notebook laptop. As laptops vary in size so much, the instructions show you how to measure yours and make a bag that fits. It's easy to resize a bag when it is made from foundation pieced plait patchwork, joined with narrow sashing strips, quilted as it is pieced. An extra layer of calico immediately under the patchwork provides sewing guidelines and careful placement of three fabrics gives the illusion of a real plait. The fourth fabric from the fat quarter quartet makes the bias binding.

Fabrics with bold modern prints and metallic highlights hint at computer graphics, while red leather handles add an unconventional yet professional look. The bag fastener is just to keep the flap closed and doesn't support any weight, so I chose an ornate, brass cloak clasp to make an unusual fastening. If a laptop bag isn't your thing, you can use the bag for books and make it the same size as mine.

Wednesday's little project

The matching drawstring pocket is simple to make and ideal for storing your laptop mouse or other little gadgets.

Patchwork method: Foundation pieced plait

More elaborate strip designs like this plait are easier to keep straight when sewn on a marked foundation. By adding a layer of wadding (batting) and calico behind the marked foundation, your patchwork is quilted as it is sewn and no more quilting is necessary unless extra decorative quilting is preferred.

1 Using Fig A, trace off a paper pattern. Go over the lines with a black pen so the lines will show through the calico. Cut three calico strips for the marked foundation panels ¼in (6mm) wider and up to ½in longer than the finished panels. Lay the calico strip over the pattern and trace through the diagonal plait guidelines with a sharp pencil. You will be able to see black pen lines quite easily through fine calico. When you reach the bottom of the paper pattern, reposition the calico strip further up the pattern and continue drawing the guidelines until the marked foundation panel is complete.

TIP

The foundation pattern in Fig A is 4in (10.2cm) wide. Line up your foundation strip using the red centre line. Your strip may be slightly narrower or wider, so trace the part of the pattern it covers. If your strips are slightly wider, extend the diagonal lines to fit.

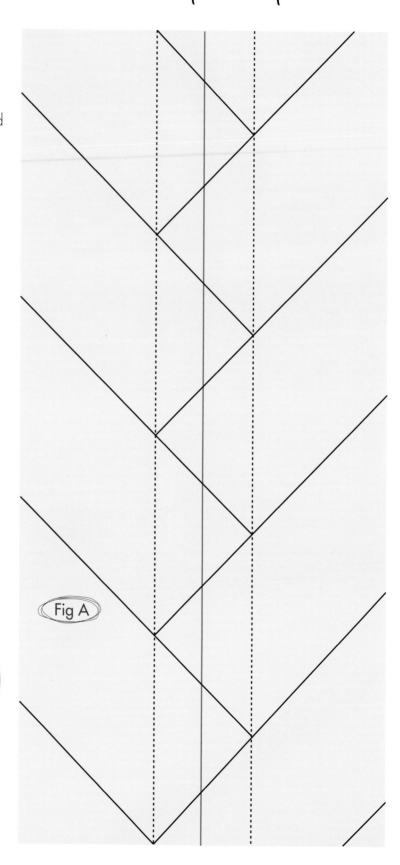

Fig A

2 Layer one plain strip of calico with one strip of wadding. Pin the marked foundation calico to the top, so the pins are visible, as shown. You will need to remove the pins as you sew the patchwork. Cut several 2in (5cm) wide strips from each of the three fabrics you want to use for the plait, parallel to the selvedge.

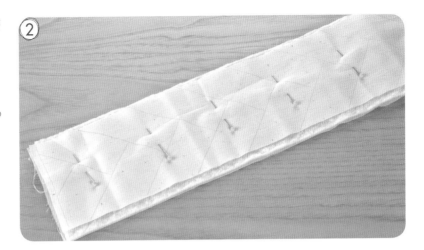

3 You can start the plait strip with any of the three fabrics. Lay the end of one strip over the end of the plait foundation, so it covers the triangle at the start of the plait, lining up its edges with the foundation lines, as shown. Pin and trim off the excess fabric at the edge.

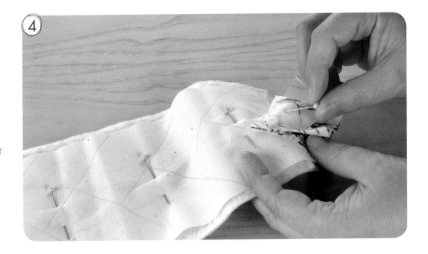

4 Choose one of the other two fabrics for the next patchwork strip. Lay it face up on the foundation, as if it were already sewn in place and trim the edge parallel with the edge of the foundation strip. Place the patch face down on the pinned triangle, lining it up with the foundation lines once again. Pin and machine sew along the long side of the strip, using the walking foot on your machine and a ¼in (6mm) seam allowance.

5 Flip over the strip you have just sewn. Finger press firmly and pin. Take the third fabric from your selection, line it up and trim it as before. It doesn't matter if the diagonal edge isn't perfectly straight, so long as the foundation strip is covered by the patchwork right up to the edge. Pin and machine sew to the foundation.

6 Flip over the third strip, finger press and pin. Continue sewing strips in the same fabric sequence – first, second and third – to create the illusion of a plait. Rather than square off the diagonal end of each strip after every piece is cut, keep that piece for the next time you use the fabric on that side of the strip, so the diagonal slopes the same way.

7 When the strip is complete, trim it to the required width using your rotary cutter. There is no need to machine sew along the edge, as the sashing strips will control the patchwork's bias edges. Make two more patchwork strips.

8 Cut a 1in (2.5cm) wide sashing strip the same length as the patchwork strip. You will need to join sashing strips to get the required length, as I did. Press the seam open. Right sides together, pin the sashing strip along the side of the patchwork strip, lining up the edges as shown. Machine sew the sashing to the patchwork, sewing a ¼in (6mm) seam using the quarter inch foot on your machine. Finger press the sashing strip away from patchwork.

9 Right sides together, pin the sashing strip to the second patchwork strip. Machine sew, using a ¼in (6mm) seam as before. Using the quarter inch foot means the left side of the foot fits snugly against the edge of the first sashing seam allowance as you sew, rather than riding over the top and pushing the seam allowance out of alignment.

10 The joined patchwork strips should lie flat, as shown. If you want a really flat finish, turn the panel over and herringbone stitch the edges of the two panels together behind the sashing strip, by hand (see diagram below).

TIP

Work herringbone stitch from left to right, going from right to left if you are left-handed. Stitches should be about ½in (1.3cm) long.

Herringbone stitch

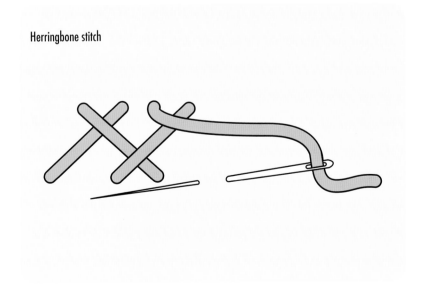

Wednesday's Projects

You Will Need

(Fabric sizes are for a smaller laptop measuring 23¾in (60.3cm) all round lengthways, 19¾in (50.2cm) all round widthways and 1¼in (3.8cm) deep.)

- Four fat quarters
- Plain calico backing and wadding (batting):
  two 9in x 2½in (22.9xm x 6.4in) pieces for bag gussets
  three 24in x 4in (61cm x 10.2cm) pieces for foundation pieced strips
- Plain calico:
  one 8½in x 4in (21.6cm x 10.2cm) piece for gadget pocket
  three 24in x 4in (61cm x 10.2cm) pieces for marked foundation panels

- One half yard (half metre) patchwork cotton for bag lining panels
- 58in x 1¼in (147.3cm x 3.2cm) wide bias binding (see Making bias binding, page 18)
- One pair 18in (45.7cm) long leather handles
- One cloak clasp or similar fastening
- 11in (27.9cm) 'rat's tail' cord or other fine cord for gadget pocket drawstrings
- Small spring toggle for cord
- Tracing paper for templates
- Double-sided sticky tape to temporarily stick handles
- Sewing threads to tone with patchwork

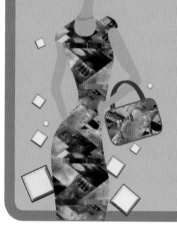

FABRIC IDEA

Two of the prints I used for the plait are quite homogenous in colour while the third had a lot of variety, so I used this one for the sashing strips for the first fabric theme. For the floral fabrics, I used the darkest mini print for the sashing. I kept the fourth fabric for the binding only each time.

Laptop Bag

Measuring the laptop

1 Begin by measuring *around* the laptop, across the length (i.e. parallel to the longest side of the screen and keyboard) and width (the shorter side), using a tape measure. Measure *across* the length and width. Measure the depth. Make a note of all the measurements. The bag should be snug but not too tight, so add a little extra, about ⅛in–¼in (3mm–6mm), to the shortest length of the bag panel and a similar amount to the side panels to allow for the wadding thickness. Add another ½in (1.3cm) to those measurements, to allow for the ¼in (6mm) bag seams on each panel. The main bag panel must be long enough to wrap around the width of the laptop with 4in–5in (10.2cm–12.7cm) extra for the bag flap. The flap will need to be larger for a deeper laptop.

Making the patchwork

2 Using the diagram and instructions on pages
50–53, make three patchwork panels (or four,
for very large laptop bags). The strips were trimmed
to measure 23in x 3¾in (58.4cm x 9.5cm). Join the
patchwork with sashing strips, as described in steps
8–10 on page 52–53. I started each patchwork
plait with a different fabric for the triangle, so
that the secondary patterns where one strip meets
another are different from the version on page 53.

Attaching the handles

3 Temporarily wrap the completed bag panel
around the laptop and pin. Position the front
handle first, clearing the lower edge of the bag
flap. Draw a short line or place a pin to indicate
the position of one end of the first handle and use a
quilter's ruler to mark the position of the other end,
which should be level with the first. Turn the bag over
and mark the position of the handle on the back,
level with the one on the front.

4 Use double-sided tape to temporarily stick the
handle tabs to the sides of the bag panel.
Stitch on the handles (see Sewing leather handles,
page 21). Round off the bag flap corners with a
2½in (6.4cm) circle template. Machine overlock or
zigzag all around the bag panel, lining up with the
marks you made in step 3.

Lining the bag panel

5 Using the bag panel as a pattern, cut a piece of lining fabric the same size as the panel. Right sides together, pin and machine sew the lining panel straight across the inside top of the bag (this is the part that will be covered by the flap end of the bag panel when the bag is finished).

6 Press the seam open, as shown. You may wish to attach the bag fastener at this stage, before the lining is sewn in place (see step 11). If you want to use hook and loop fastening tape instead (see 'Idea' page 58), it must be sewn in place now.

7 Fold the lining fabric behind the bag panel and pin together around the edge. Machine sew all around the panel, ⅛in (3mm) from the edge, including topstitching across the previously sewn seam.

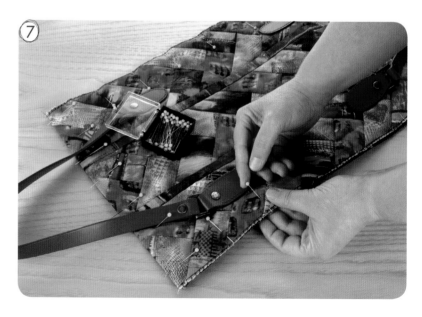

Making the side gussets

8 Pin the bag panel around the laptop again and measure from the straight top seam under the bag flap to the bottom of the bag, where it goes around the lower edge of the laptop. Add ¼in (6mm) and cut two strips to this length. The strip measurement will equal the laptop depth plus ½in (1.3cm) for the seam allowance and ⅛in–¼in (3–6mm) for ease. I cut my side strips 9⅛in x 2½in (23.2cm x 6.4cm). Use a circle template the same diameter as the strip width and make a curve at one end of the strip.

Layer each strip with a piece of wadding (batting) and backing fabric and quilt some parallel lines. Pin one gusset strip to one side of the bag panel to check the length, beginning with the curve at the bottom and easing the bag panel around the curve, as shown. Remember that the finished gusset will be ¼in (6mm) shorter once the lining is sewn across the top of the gusset. Cut the gusset slightly shorter, if necessary. Cut the second gusset to match. Use the gussets as patterns to cut two lining strips from the lining fabric.

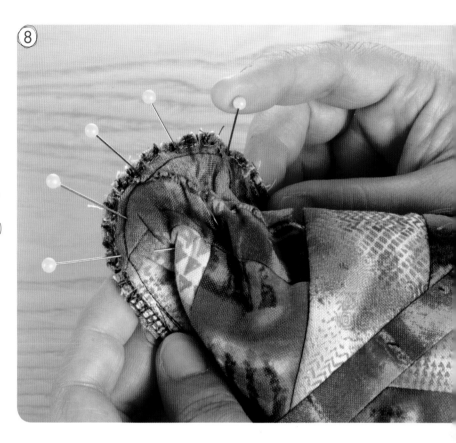

9 Right sides together, pin and machine sew one gusset strip to one lining strip, across the straight end. Press the seam and fold the lining against the back of the gusset, as you did with the lining fabric and bag panel. Machine sew all around the panel, ⅛in (3mm) from the edge, including topstitching across the previously sewn seam. Repeat with the other gusset strip. Clip around the straight sections to go around the curves at the corners of the bag panels and each end of the gusset strip, clipping about ⅛in (3mm) in from the panel edge, so you can ease one section to the other at these points.

Pin and machine sew one gusset strip to each side of the bag, lining up the straight top of the gusset with the straight top of the bag panel (underneath the flap).

Completing the bag

10 Make bias binding from the fourth fabric and pin to the outside of the bag, leaving approx. ¾in (1.9cm) extra binding at each end. Ease the bias binding around the curved corners on the bag flap. Turn the work over and machine sew with the binding underneath, so you can line your stitches up on top of the previous stitching, exactly ¼in (6mm) from the edge. Turn in the ends of the binding and stitch in place (see page 18). Turn under the binding so it is a snug fit to the edge and slipstitch all round.

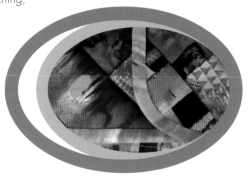

11 Attach the fastener to the bag. Begin by sewing the hook part of the cloak clasp (or similar fastener) to the centre of the flap, then use it to position the loop section by temporarily fastening the clasp and marking where the loop part should be sewn. Take care not to stitch through the bag lining.

IDEA

For a streamlined style, you may prefer an invisible fastening with hook and loop tape. You need to position and machine sew the tape before the lining is sewn to the main panel (steps 5–7), to avoid visible stitching on the outside of the bag flap. One strip should be sewn to the patchwork panel and the other to the lining under the bag flap.

A Garland of flowers

This floral theme is a more relaxed look if you're off to a creative writing course or poetry group. I used the same leather handles, this time in brown, and the same brass fastener. This fat quarter bundle had three coordinating floral prints with different predominant colours and pattern densities — enough contrast to show the plait design well. The matching floral braid was a lucky find and is hand sewn to the bag flap once the bag is complete.

Gadget Pocket

Making the patchwork

1 Using the diagram and instructions on pages 50–53, make one patchwork panel the same size as the piece in Fig A on page 50 – 4in x 8½in (10.2cm x 21.6cm). Leave out the wadding layer and use just one layer of calico behind the patchwork, to reduce bulk for this smaller bag. Cut one 4in x 8½in (10.2cm x 21.6cm) piece for lining and two 4½in x 1½in (11.4 x 3.8cm) pieces for drawstring channels from one of the patchwork fabrics.

2 Fold the patchwork panel in half, right sides together, and machine sew the side seams with a ¼in (6mm) seam allowance, as shown. Fold the lining piece the same way and sew the side seams with the same seam allowance, but leave about 3in (7.5cm) unsewn in one side seam. Turn under a ¼in (6mm) doubled hem at each end of the 4½in x 11½in (11.4cm x 3.8cm) pieces for the drawstring channels.

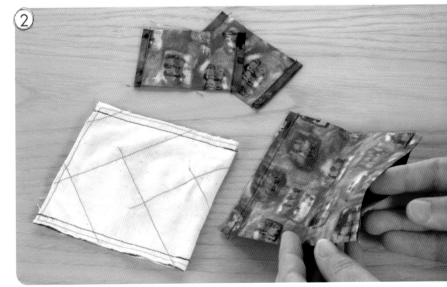

3 Turn the patchwork bag right side out.
Fold each drawstring channel in half.
Pin one folded channel to the top of each side of
the bag, lining up the raw edges with the top
of the bag.

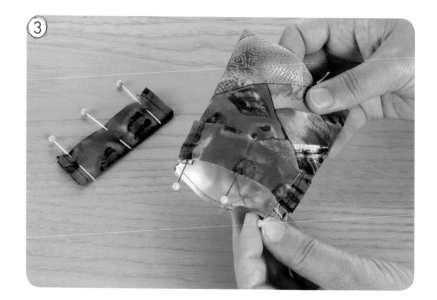

4 The bag lining should remain turned inside
out, with the seams on the outside. Place the
patchwork bag outer inside the bag lining. Align
the side seams on the bag and the lining, line up the
tops of both and pin around the top, as shown.

TIP

*Machine sewing around a narrow
cylinder, like the top of this bag, is easier if
you sew with the presser foot against the inside
of the bag, rather than trying to fit the cylinder
around the machine's free arm.*

5 Machine sew around the top of the bag,
stitching the lining to the outside of the
bag. The drawstring channels are stitched into this
seam at the top of the bag, although at the moment
they are hidden between the bag lining and outer.
Slip your fingers inside the gap in the lining seam
and take hold of the bag outer.

6 Carefully turn the whole bag right sides out through the gap in the lining seam. When the bag is turned through, push the lining back down into the bag, as shown. Push the lining corners down into the corners of the bag, making sure they are well turned out. Slipstitch the lining gap closed.

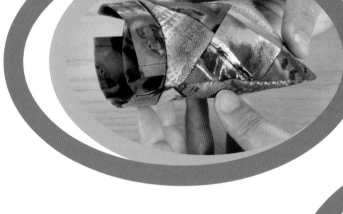

7 Thread the rat's tail cord through both channels from left to right and back again. Thread both ends through a spring toggle before knotting the ends. Alternatively, use two lengths of cord and thread the second from right to left. Finish the end of the cord with a padded bobble over the knot, cutting a 3½in (8.9cm) circle and following the instructions for the Eclipse Evening Bag (step 13, page 44).

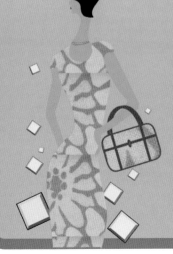

FABRIC IDEA

Faded reds, soft peaches and pale greens are good for a vintage, worn and washed look. The tone-on-tone print could be used for the binding, while there is ample contrast in the other three fabrics to make the plait patchwork look fresh. Try cutting across a stripe if you think it will be difficult to keep it straight in the patchwork or cut the stripe pieces on the bias.

Typo Satchel
and Book Bag

Thursday's trip to work needs superwoman efficiency so make sure you look the part with this attractive and practical satchel. The standard QWERTY keyboard on the satchel flap is made from scrap-booking brads with alphabet 'keys' echoing the keyboard layout on offset patchwork squares, which are easily made using Seminole patchwork techniques.

I chose black and cream fabrics with handwriting, engraving and pinstripe themes. These included a large-scale print and an ombre woven plaid for extra variety in the 1in (2.5cm) squares, a directional print and a woven stripe. Chunky silver buckles, eyelets and floral paperclips used as embellishments add a chic touch. The side panels are tied across inside for security and there are pockets on each end – handy for tickets or your sunglasses.

Thursday's little project
The matching book bag is perfect for something sensational to read on the train and fits inside the Typo Satchel with room to spare. It fastens with a matching buckle so your book doesn't have to be a super snug fit to stay in place.

Patchwork method: Seminole slices

Machine sewing strips together, cutting slices from the patchwork and then rearranging them is the basis of Seminole patchwork, originating with the North American Seminole Indians. It is much easier to sew strips and cut them than to start out with a heap of fiddly 1½in (3.8cm) squares.

1 Cut 1½in (3.8cm) wide strips from each fabric – exact cutting lists are included in the instructions for the Typo Satchel and the Book Bag (page 66). Arrange these strips according to Fig B on page 69. Machine sew the strips together in pairs, then sew one pair to another until that patchwork set is complete. Note that some sets of patchwork strips include narrower 1in (2.5cm) wide strips at the ends, to achieve the offset squares pattern. Press seams in the same direction along the strip.

FABRIC IDEA

Using only five fabrics means that they need to be versatile to give this design plenty of variety. Stripes can run horizontally or vertically, as can directional patterns. Ombre fabrics have shading effects so patches look like they have been cut from different but related fabrics. High or low tonal contrast works just fine.

2 Using your rotary cutter and ruler, cut slices across the patchwork pieces. As the finished size of the squares in this design is 1in (2.5cm) and the width of the strips was 1½in (3.8cm), these slices need to be 1½in (3.8cm) wide.

3 For the Typo Satchel, arrange the strips following the order shown in Fig C (page 69), or another order if you prefer, making sure the squares are offset from one row to the next – like a brick wall. Take care to pin the strips so that the squares interlock neatly. Machine sew the strips together in pairs, then sew one pair to another until each part of the patchwork is complete, again following the number of rows shown in Fig C.

4 The buckle and eyelet straps are also inserted as part of the patchwork, giving the bag a streamlined look and enabling the straps to be sewn in with the quilting as well as the patchwork, so they are attached to the bag's structure at several points. The strap is centred on the patchwork panel, as described for each bag, and the raw edge of the strap sticks out beyond the patchwork by 1in (2.5cm), as shown.

5 Machine sew the seam and press the seam allowance so the strap points in the desired direction, with the overlap section lying over the patchwork seam next to the one where it is sewn. When this is machine quilted in the ditch, the stitches will go through the strap on two seams, not just one.

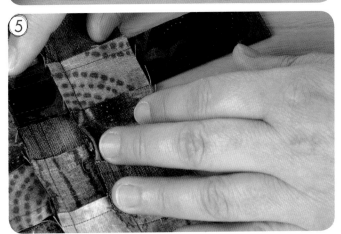

TIP
Pin long strips carefully before machine sewing, starting with a pin at each end at right angles to the strip and adding more pins along the length. If you machine long strips without pinning first, the ends will almost always be out of alignment.

6 The finished strap lies neatly in the correct direction. Add eyelets after the bag is completed, so you can check the best position for them against the exact position of the buckle.

Thursday's Projects

You Will Need

- Five fat quarters
- One 11½in x 3¾in (29.2cm x 9.5cm) piece of denim or canvas for Typo Satchel base
- Plain calico backing and wadding (batting):
  one 26½in x 12in (67.3cm x 30.5cm) piece for Typo Satchel panel
  two 7in x 5in (17.8cm x 12.7cm) pieces for Typo Satchel pockets
  one 10in x 13in (25.4cm x 33cm) piece for Book Bag panel
- Cotton quilting fabric for lining:
  one 25.75in x 11in (65.4cm x 27.9cm) piece for Typo Satchel
  one 9in x 12½in (22.9cm x 31.8cm) piece for Book Bag
- 94in x 1¼in (238.8cm x 3.2cm) wide bias binding (see Making bias binding page 18)
- Buckles for 1in (2.5cm) wide straps:
  three for Typo Satchel
  one for Book Bag
- ¼in (6mm) eyelets, to match buckle metal:
  eight for Typo Satchel
  two for Book Bag
- Full alphabet of typewriter key/alphabet brads or button collection
- Fancy paperclips or other embellishments
- Tracing paper for side panel pattern
- Circle templates to draft pattern
- Eyelet setting tools
- Sewing and quilting threads to tone with patchwork

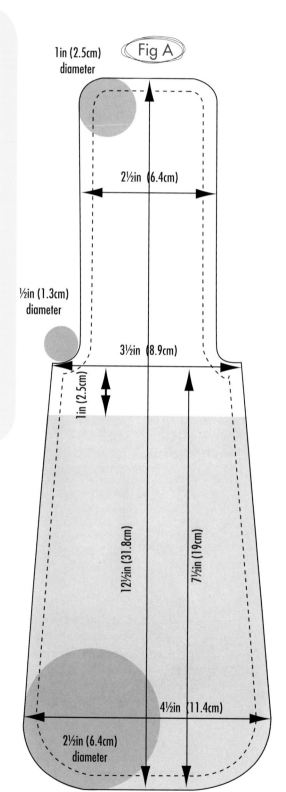

Fig A

1in (2.5cm) diameter

2½in (6.4cm)

½in (1.3cm) diameter

3½in (8.9cm)

1in (2.5cm)

12½in (31.8cm)

7½in (19cm)

4½in (11.4cm)

2½in (6.4cm) diameter

Typo Satchel

Constructing the side panels

1 Because the side panels and pockets use the larger pieces of fabric, it is a good idea to cut these first. Draft a paper pattern of the pieces shown in Fig A – the side panel is the whole shape outlined while the pocket is shaded in grey. Cut four side panels (two lining and two outer fabric) and four pocket panels (two lining and two outer fabric).

Tack a piece of wadding (batting) behind the two outer pocket panels and trim its edge to line up with the fabric. If you wish, each side panel and pocket could be cut from a different fabric, as I did, with the two lightest fabrics for the side panels and linings and the stripe for the pocket, lined with the black polka dot, or you can use the same fabric for each panel. The pocket lining can use up the fat quarter that has been cut diagonally to make the bias binding strips (see page 18) as the diagonal seam won't be visible when the bag is finished.

2 Cut two 1in x 12½in (2.5cm x 31.8cm) strips and make two thin ties, following instructions for making a closed end strap (page 19). The finished ties will be just ¼in (6mm) wide. Pin one of the ties to the top of one of the side panels, so that the raw end sticks out over the seam allowance by an extra ³⁄₈in (1cm). Pin this side panel and one of the lining panels right sides together around the top of the panel and machine stitch, trapping the end of the tie in the seam allowance at the top. Turn the panel right side out – gently pulling on the tie helps you do this – and press. Top stitch by machine around the seam, stitching ⅛in (3mm) from the edge.

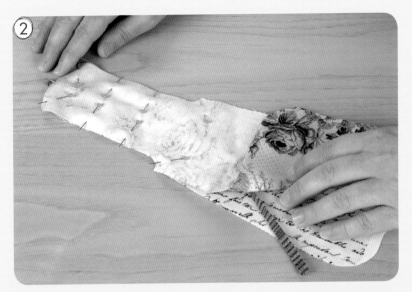

TIP

I made my straps from two fabrics, the stripe and the ombre weave, but you can use two, three or more fabrics for added variety. Don't cut all your straps from one fabric, or you won't have enough left for the patchwork!

Making the handle and straps

3 To make the straps, cut 4in (10.2cm) wide strips along the fabric grain for minimum stretch. The satchel handle needs to be 40in (101.6cm) long, so piece this from three shorter sections, sewn together at 45-degree angles, a buckle and one 5in (12.7cm) long strip for the eyelet strap.

Make the buckle straps following the instructions on page 19 and the eyelet strap following the instructions for the Closed end strap (page 19). The handle is made with both ends closed and a strap pad made from 8½in (21.6cm) long pieces – one 21½in (6.4cm) wide and two 1¼in (3.8cm). See strap pad instructions, page 20.

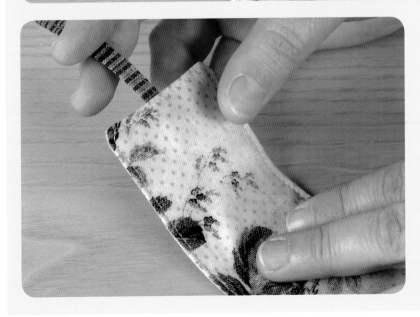

Making the side pockets

4 Using an awl, narrow scissor points, large bodkin or similar, make a hole in one of the 4in (10.2cm) side buckle straps. Position it in the middle of the strap width but offset from the centre of the strap length by ¼in (6mm), so one end of the strap will overhang the other, reducing bulk in the finished bag. Try to prise the fabric fibres apart just enough to thread the buckle's prong on to the strap, without cutting the threads if possible. Checking that the buckle is the right way round on the strap (the prong should be pointing upwards on the finished strap), position the buckle strap at the centre top of the pocket panel, with the raw ends overlapping the edge by ³⁄₈in (1cm).

5 Right sides together, pin the pocket lining to the pocket, as shown, with the buckle strap sticking out across the top. Machine sew across the top of the pocket. Press the seam open and fold the lining behind the pocket, so the buckle strap is standing up at the top of the pocket.

6 Topstitch three lines across the top of the pocket, ⅛in (3mm) apart, as shown. Pin the completed pocket panel to one of the side panels and machine sew together ⅛in (3mm) from the edge, to complete one side panel. Repeat for the other side panel.

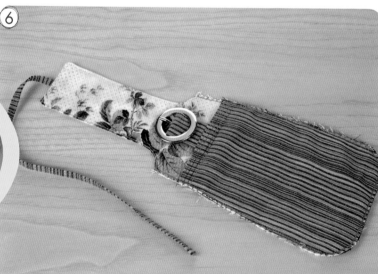

Making the patchwork bag panel

7 Using all five of your fabrics, cut the following 1½in (3.8cm) strips – nine 4½in (11.4cm) strips from four of the fabrics and eight from the remaining one, plus four 7½in (19cm) strips from three fabrics, five from one and three from the remaining one. This will give plenty of variety to the patchwork strips. I cut the striped fabric so the stripes go along the 7½in (19cm) strips but across the 4½in (11.4cm) strips, with the cream 'script' running at right angles to this. Cut four 7½in x 1in (19cm x 2.5cm) strips for the ends of the 7½in (19cm) panels.

Arrange and sew the pieces so you have four 11½in x 4½in (29.2cm x 11.4cm) panels and two 11½in x 7½in (29.2cm x 19cm) panels. I arranged my strips from light to dark as shown in Fig B. This is just a suggestion, you may prefer to arrange your strips in a different order.

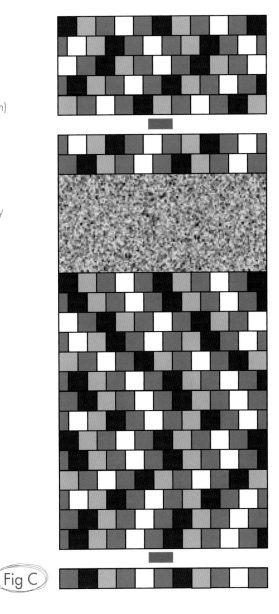

Fig C

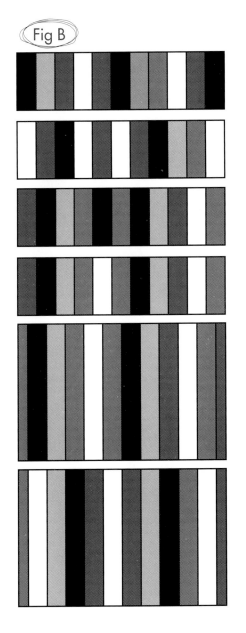

Fig B

8 Cut the patchwork panels into 1½in (3.8cm) wide strips, as shown on page 64. Arrange the strips for the bag panel. Fig C shows how I arranged my strips, but you may want to play around with the arrangement to suit your fabrics. The squares make a random pattern that looks complex. Don't worry about the same fabrics being in adjacent squares – these duos and trios give the patchwork a sense of rhythm. Machine sew the patchwork together, sewing the strips into pairs, then sewing one pair to another until the patchwork is complete (see step 3, page 65).

Sew the 11½in x 3¾in (29.2cm x 9.5cm) piece of denim or canvas into the patchwork as shown in Fig C. Sew the rows where there is a gap in the diagram last, inserting the buckle strap and eyelet strap into the patchwork as indicated by the red lines. Press the seams, checking that the patchwork panel is square and the seams with the straps inserted are pressed in the same direction as the ends of the straps (see step 6, page 65).

9 Layer the backing fabric, wadding and patchwork panel (see Making the quilt sandwich, page 14). Machine quilt in the ditch along each continuous row and stitch around the panel, about ⅛in (3mm) from the edge. Using a 2½in (6.4cm) circle template, draw and cut the curved corners on the flap end of the bag panel. Arrange the typewriter key brads or buttons – follow the QWERTY keyboard layout as shown here and in the photo on page 63. The bottom row of letters is the fourth fabric row from the end of the bag flap. If you have number 'keys', you can add these too, beginning with '1' to the top left of the 'Q' key.

10 Brads are made from quite soft metal and have prongs on the back. Mark the centre of each square with a cross, make a small hole using a bodkin or awl, push the brad through and open up the prongs on the back with a blunt knife blade or old pair of scissors. You may wish to add another piece of fabric across the back of the 'keyboard' section, to protect the bag lining from the brads or, if the brads are small enough for you to machine quilt between them, add the brads before layering and quilting.

11 Sew on the extra embellishments by hand. The floral paperclips I used make great embellishments and are easy to attach with a few stitches. Match your thread colour as closely as possible to the embellishment and use strong or doubled thread. Take a good look at your embellishment pieces and work out the most efficient and unobtrusive way to stitch them on to the patchwork panel. Keep them 1in (2.5cm) away from the panel edges, so they don't interfere with assembling the bag.

IDEA

Many brads and decorations sold for scrapbooking are robust enough for use as a quilting embellishment. Do some lateral thinking – almost anything that can be sewn or fastened on can be used to embellish. I spotted the floral paperclips in a stationery store!

Completing the satchel

12 With the patchwork panel and the lining back to back, stitch the panel to the lining ⅛in (3mm) from the edge. If necessary, sew two pieces of fabric together for the lining. Zigzag or overlock the edge. Pin one of the side panels to the completed bag panel, lining up the centre bottom edge of the side panel with the centre of the bag base strip and the 'shoulder' of the side panel with the top of the seventh patchwork row. Work upwards from the base on the front and the back (this is the top of the front part of the bag panel). Clip the bag panel to ease it around the side panel's curved corners. Pin the other side panel in place and machine sew the side panels to the bag.

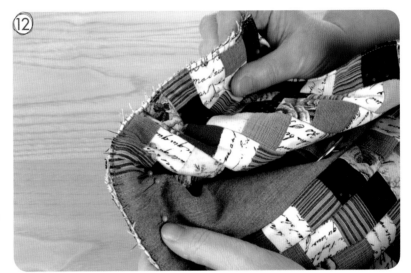

13 Sew bias binding to finish off the raw edges. Pin the bias binding to the outside of the bag, leaving approx. ¾in (1.9cm) extra binding at each end. Ease the bias binding around the curved bottom corners. Turn the work over and machine sew with the binding underneath, so that you can line your stitches up on top of the previous stitching, exactly ¼in (6mm) from the edge. Turn in the ends of the binding and stitch in place (see page 18). Turn under the binding so it is a snug fit to the edge and slipstitch all round.

14 Position and set the eyelets, using your eyelet setting tools (see page 7). The three eyelets on the strap are set 1in (2.5cm) apart, beginning 2in (5cm) from each end. To line up the eyelets for the buckle strap, lay the strap over the buckle and decide where you want the first eyelet inserted – ⁵⁄₈in (1.6cm) from where the strap joins the bag is about right, but it might depend on your buckle. The second eyelet is ⁵⁄₈in (1.6cm) from the first.

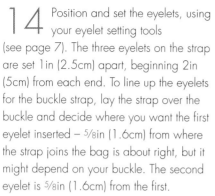

Taupe tranquillity

Taupe fabrics capture the natural look perfectly and the lower tonal contrast calms the busy squares patchwork. This time the stripe is very subtle with a hand-woven look and the prints are all large scale for lots of variety. I used the same denim for the base of the bag, but the soft brown colours give it a warmer feeling. Bronzed metal buckles always look good with browns – antique gold would also work well. However, bronze isn't so easy to find for eyelets, so these are black enamel, which coordinates well.

I collected wooden buttons from quilt shops and specialist button retailers and had fun arranging them on the bag, grouping them together to create little stories – the cat with the fish, a flower with foliage, watering can and flower in pot and so on. The buttons were sewn on to the panels after quilting, so they didn't obstruct the machine foot.

Book Bag

Making the straps

1 To make the straps, cut 4in (10.2cm) wide strips, along the fabric grain for minimum stretch. You need two pieces 11in long (28in) for the bag handles, one 5in (12.7cm) long for the buckle and one 6in (15.6cm) long for the eyelet strap. Make the buckle strap and handles following the instructions for the basic strap and eyelet strap following the instructions for the closed end strap (page 19).

Making the panels

2 Cut two pocket panels for inside the bag – 9in x 11½in (22.9cm x 29.2cm) for the back pocket and 9in (22.9cm) square for the front. Fold in half with the right side on the outside, so each panel measures 9in (22.9cm) tall, and machine sew down the folded edge, ⅛in (3mm) from the edge. Alternatively, make each pocket from two pieces, 6in (15.6cm) wide for the back pocket and 5in (12.7cm) for the front. The two pieces for each pocket don't have to be the same fabric.

3 Cut thirty-two 4½in x 1½in (11.4cm x 3.8cm) strips, six from each fabric in the fat quarter plus two extra from whatever fabric you like. Now cut four 4½in x 1in (11.4cm x 2.5cm) strips. You can construct some of the patchwork from 1½in (3.8cm) squares if fabric is running out. Assemble four patchwork panels with eight 1½in (3.8cm) strips sewn together with a 1in (2.5cm) strip on one end, arranging the strips in a random sequence. Cut 1½in (3.8cm) slices from these panels and arrange them to make the bag panel, as shown opposite.

Machine sew the patchwork strips together (see step 8 on page 69) and add the strap for the buckle two rows back from one end and the strap for the eyelet one row back from the other. Layer the backing fabric, wadding and patchwork panel (see Making the quilt sandwich, page 14). Machine quilt in the ditch along each continuous row and stitch around the panel, about ⅛in (3mm) from the edge. Add the embellishments.

Constructing the book bag

4 Arrange and pin the handles to each end of the bag, setting the outer edge of the handles 2¼in (5.7cm) in from the long edges (this will line up one end of the strap directly on a patchwork square, while the other end will be over two squares) so the raw ends overhang the panel by ¼in (6mm). Place the pinheads pointing outwards from the bag edge, so you can remove them easily later.

5 Right sides together, pin the front and back pockets in place along the ends of the bag panel only, making sure the wider pocket is on the part of the panel with the eyelet strap – this will be the back when a book is in the bag. Right sides together, pin the 9in x 12½in (22.9cm x 31.8cm) lining fabric to the ends of the bag, so the front and back pockets are sandwiched between the bag panel and the lining.

6 Machine sew along both ends of the bag, but not across the top or bottom, to make a tube, with the pockets inside. Put your hand inside the completed tube and, holding the pocket panels, turn it right side out. The book bag will look like a tube with the pocket panels sticking out at each side. Press, gently pulling the pocket panels outwards.

7 Lay the book bag with the outer panel face down. Fold the pocket panels over on to the lining and pin across the top and bottom of the bag, through all the layers. They will now look like pockets. Machine sew, 1/8in (3mm) from the edge. Sew bias binding to finish off the raw edges. Pin the bias binding to the outside of the bag, leaving approx. 3/4in (1.9cm) extra binding at each end and complete, following the instructions in step 13 (page 71) and Making bias binding (page 18).

8 Position and set the two eyelets, using your eyelet setting tools (see page 7). To line up the eyelets for the buckle strap, lay the strap over the buckle and decide where you want the first eyelet inserted – 1 7/8 in (4.8cm) from where the strap joins the bag is about right, but it might depend on the size of your buckle and how thick your books are! The second eyelet is 1/2in (1.3cm) from the first.

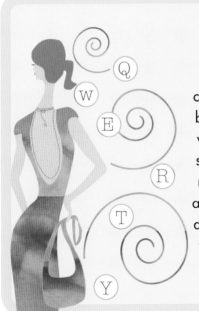

FABRIC IDEA

Perhaps muted tones aren't your thing, so try a colourful patchwork with batiks. Marbled and shaded batiks or other hand-dyed fabrics give a wonderful variety of colours and tones from just one fabric, so using five of these luscious cottons would make a vibrant patchwork, full of sunshine and a holiday mood. Try embroidering lazy daisies with shaded embroidery threads on your patchwork squares as an alternative to buttons or brads.

Swag Bag
and Curvy Coin Purse

Indulge in a little retail therapy on Friday and visit a farmers' market. The pretty, shabby chic style of the Swag Bag and Curvy Coin Purse is perfect for a shopping trip in the fresh air. The radiating patchwork is rotary cut with paper templates positioned under the ruler. It looks sophisticated but is quick and easy to make. The panels are quilted in the ditch with a fancy machine stitch down the centre of each strip.

A gathered base strip, the ideal place to use a striped fabric, adds feminine style and is pleated into the ends of the strap. The wide integral strap and zip strip link the two bag panels making a casual shoulder bag edged with bias binding. Twin lace strips appear to make continuous loops, adding a pretty finishing touch.

Friday's little project

The Curvy Coin Purse shape repeats the patchwork design of the Swag Bag and has plenty of room for loose change.

76

Patchwork method: Rotary cutting with templates

Combining rotary cutting with templates speeds up the cutting process, allowing you to cut through several layers at once. More complex shapes become easy. Tracing paper is translucent so you can see the fabric pattern through the paper.

1 Copy and enlarge by 125 per cent the templates in Fig B on page 80 and cut them out, using scissors suitable for paper (not your best sewing scissors!). Lay out four fat quarters – two with the right side facing down and two with the right side facing up. Flip alternate templates over – you will cut mirror images of these. Arrange the templates, lining up the centre arrows with the fabric grain. Pin each template securely through all four layers (the photo shows cutting using the Swag Bag templates only), using fine pins with small heads or flat-headed flower pins, not glass-headed pins. With the templates as a guide, line up your rotary cutter and cut all the straight sides first, turning your cutting mat as necessary and cutting one stack of templates

2 Using your fabric scissors, trim each stack of patches, cutting the curved edges right up to the edge of the template. The points of the templates are trimmed off as necessary on the template page, so the patches will align neatly. Handle the patches carefully, as the edges are off grain and can be easily stretched.

3 Remove the pins. You will have one of each
piece in each fabric required to make the two
bag panels. Arrange the fabrics in the following
sequence – fabric 1, then 2, 3, 4 and back to 1.
The side panels will each have a different sequence
and no two pieces will share the same fabric and
the same shape. Fig A shows the layout for the
patchwork pieces for half of the panel – the other
half is a mirror image.

Fig A

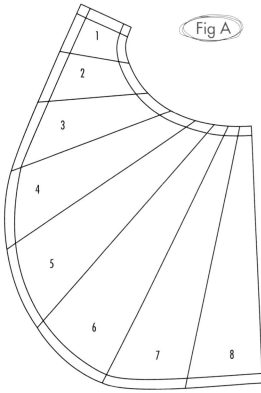

1
2
3
4
5
6
7
8

FABRIC IDEA

Try including patterns in different sizes, with
directional patterns or striped motifs, in your
fabric selection. Use a small-scale print for
bias binding strips and a striped design for
the gathered bag base and purse gusset.

4 Working around the 'sunburst' shape,
pin patches together in pairs, machine
sew with a ¼in (6mm) seam, then join one pair
to the next and so on, until the panel is complete.
The template points are trimmed as necessary so it
will be easy to line them up for sewing. Press all the
seams to one side.

Friday's Projects

You Will Need

- Six fat quarters
- Plain calico backing and wadding (batting):
  one 38in x 3in (96.5cm x 7.6cm)
  strip for bag strap
  two 13½in x 10in (34.3cm x 25.4cm)
  pieces for bag side panels
  one 11in x 3in (27.9cm x 7.6cm)
  strip for purse gusset
  two 6in x 41½in (15.3cm x 11.4cm)
  pieces for purse side panels

- Cotton quilting fabric for lining:
  one 38in x 3in (96.5cm x 7.6cm) strip for
  bag strap
  two 13½in x 10in (34.3cm x 25.4cm)
  pieces for bag side panels

  one 42in x 4in (106.7cm x 10.2cm)
  strip for bag gusset
  one 11in x 3in (27.9cm x 7.6cm)
  strip for purse gusset
  two 6in x 4½in (15.3cm x 11.4cm)
  pieces for purse side panels

- 132in x 1in (335.3cm x 2.5cm) lace edging or ³/₈in (1cm)
  wide braid
- 125in x 1¼in (317.5cm x 3.2cm) bias
  binding (see Making bias binding, page18)
- One 12in (30cm) zip, for bag
- One 4in (10.2cm) zip, for purse
- Tracing paper for making templates
- Sewing and quilting threads to tone
  with patchwork

Swag bag
Making the panels

1 Using four of your fabrics, cut out and sew two patchwork side panels, using the templates Fig A and Fig B and following the instructions on pages 78–79. Layer the backing fabric, wadding and patchwork panel for each side panel (see Making the quilt sandwich, page 14). Machine quilt in the ditch along each seam line and stitch around the panel, about ⅛in (3mm) from the edge.

IDEA
Choose a lace or braid trim that compliments the style of your fabrics, such as the creamy cotton lace used for the blue, cream and red bag, or try accenting a colour in the print, like the orange and gold braid on the blue bag duo, shown on page 86.

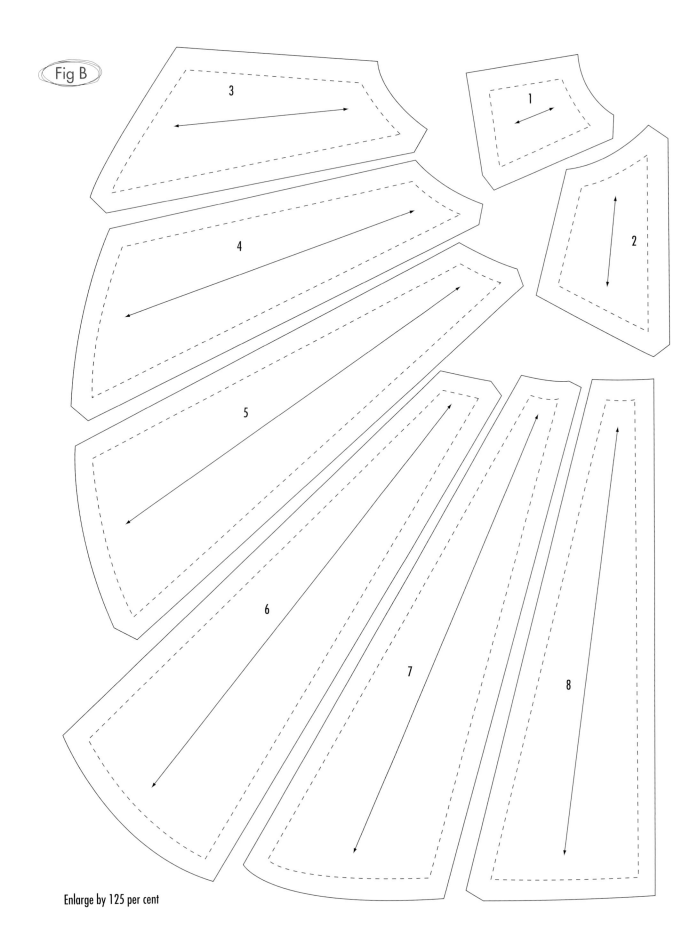

2 Draw a line down the centre of each patchwork piece and machine quilt down this line using one of the fancy stitches on your machine. Trim the backing and wadding (batting) to the edge of the patchwork panel and zigzag or machine overlock right round the panel. Position lace or other trim, pin and machine or hand sew, as appropriate – the lace edge is ⅛in (3mm) from the edge of the side panel, so it will lie under the bias binding when the bag is finished. Using the side panels as patterns, cut out tlining fabric to size. Keep the lining pieces separate until step 7.

3 Using one of your fabrics with a stripe or linear design, if you have one like this, cut out one piece measuring 21in x 4in (53.3cm x 10.2cm) and two pieces 11in (27.9cm) long, tapering from 4in (10.2cm) wide at one end to 2½in (6.4cm) at the other. See Fig C. Right sides together, machine sew one tapered piece to each end of the straight strip to make the bag gusset and press seams to one side. Using the completed bag gusset as your pattern, pin to the lining fabric and cut out the lining to the same shape. Stitch gusset and lining together ⅛in (3mm) from the edge and zigzag or overlock.

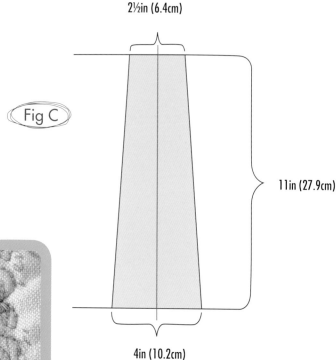

2½in (6.4cm)

Fig C

11in (27.9cm)

4in (10.2cm)

IDEA

Many modern sewing machines have attractive embroidery stitch patterns or decorative utility stitches. Select one that you like – I used a floral scroll pattern on my machine. Some machines have dozens of patterns to choose from! Alternatively, quilt these lines with an embroidery stitch.

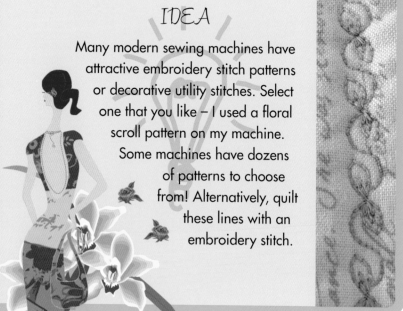

TIP

Don't stint on the pins – use plenty to control the gathers and stitch slowly, so that the fabric is evenly eased under the machine foot, not pushed into clumps and bumps.

Constructing the bag

4 Loosen the machine's top tension to zero and, with the longest possible stitch length, sew a gathering thread along each side of the gusset, about ⅛in (3mm) from the edge, leaving the ends long enough to hold and gather. Place pins on either side of the gusset, at the centre and 4½in (11.4cm) from each end. These will line up with the dots on the edge of the bag panel diagram (Fig B, page 80), on the seam between patch three and four.

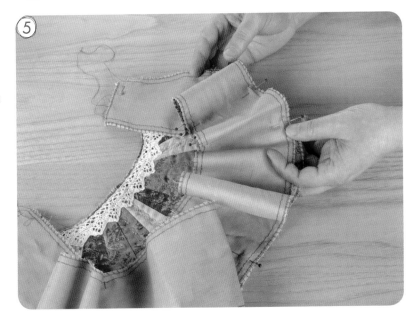

5 Line up the gusset with the first side panel, outer fabrics together, lining up the pins at the 4½in (11.4cm) point from the top of the side panel and at the centre bottom edge of the side panel, going around the curve. Gently pulling on the gathering thread that looks tightest, begin gathering up the gusset to match the edge of the side panel.

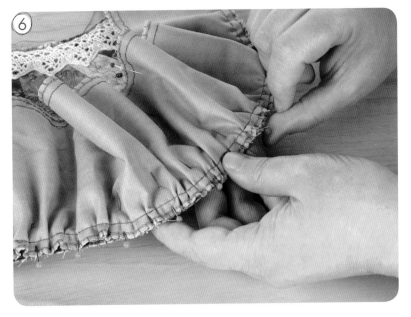

6 Smooth out the gathers as you work, so that they are nice and even. Hold them in place by pinning at right angles to the panel edge, with the pin heads on the outside, as shown, and fasten off the gathering threads by twisting in a figure of eight around the pins at each end.

7 With the right side of the bag lining against the bag gusset lining, pin the lining panel to the side panel and gusset, working around the edge, sandwiching the gathered gusset between the side panel and the lining. Take care that the edges are lined up accurately. Machine stitch around the outside edge of the side panel, sewing through the gathered and lined gusset and the bag lining. Keep the gathers neat and remove each pin as you come to it. Put your hand in between the side panel and lining, take hold of the gusset and turn the bag right side out. Repeat to attach the other side panel and lining piece.

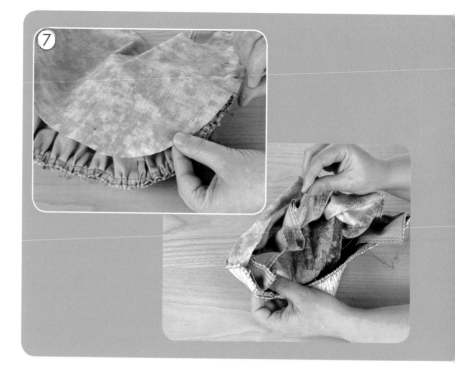

8 Line up the top edge of the lining with the top edge of the bag on each side, pin and tack (baste) the edges together, about 3/8in (1cm) from the edge. Press around the base of the bag, going around the gusset seam but taking care not to squash the gathers.

9 Make a box pleat at each side of the top of the bag, as shown, so that the gusset fabric goes into the pleat, and tack (baste) to hold the pleat in place. The width of the top of the bag at this point should now measure 2½in (6.4cm).

Making the strap and zip strip

10 Cut thirty-six 2½in x 1½in (6.4cm x 3.8cm) pieces, seven from each of the four fabrics used to make the side panel and eight from the fabric used for the bias binding. Arrange these in a sequence of all five fabrics, starting and finishing with the bias binding fabric. Machine sew the long sides together to make a patchwork strip measuring 36½in x 2½in (92.7cm x 6.4cm). Press the seams in one direction. Layer the backing fabric, wadding and patchwork strip (see Making the quilt sandwich, page 14). Quilt in the ditch between each patch. Position lace or other trim as before, pin and machine or hand sew, as appropriate.

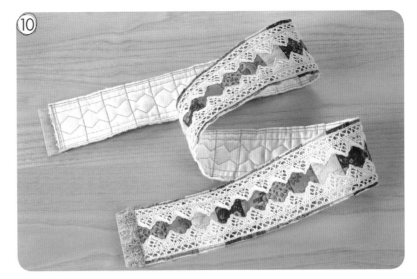

11 Cut two pieces of fabric 2½in x 1in (6.4cm x 2.5cm) and piece to each end of the strip, to join the strap to the bag. Using a strip like this to join the bag and the strap together is a good way to avoid unnecessary and hard-to-stitch bulk at this point in the bag design. It will give the illusion that the lace or braid is passing behind the strip and going around the top of the bag in a continuous loop, but without any problems disguising the starting and finishing point!

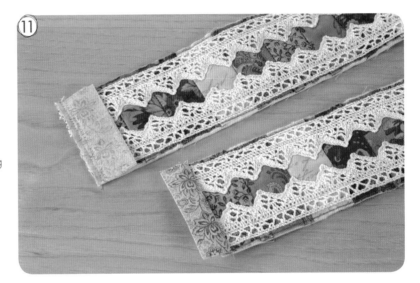

12 Right sides together, line up the ends of the strap strip with the top ends of the bag and pin. Machine sew together – adding an extra line of stitching if you wish – inside the seam allowance. Press towards the joining strips at the end of the bag strap. Cut two 12½in x 1½in (31.8cm x 3.2cm) strips from the lining fabric and two from one of the bag fabrics. Make the zip strip following the instructions on page 16.

Completing the bag

13 Make a strip to line the bag strap section by cutting two or more strips 2½in (6.4cm) wide from one of the patchwork fabrics, piecing together like patchwork and cutting the length to measure 37in (94cm) long. Right sides together, machine sew this strip to each end of the zip strip, to make a loop.

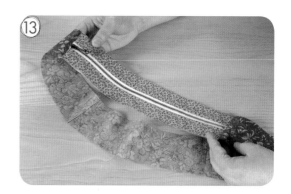

14 Line up the seam at the end of the zip strip with the seam linking the joining strip at each end of the strap to the bag. Line up the edges of the zip strip and strap lining loop made in step 16 with the edges of the bag and the edges of the strap, easing the zip strip section to the inside of the curved top edge of the bag. Clip the top edge of the bag, approx. ⅛in (3mm) in, all along the edge to help you do this. Machine sew each side of the loop to the bag, stitching ¼in (6mm) from the edge.

15 Sew bias binding to finish off the raw edges. Pin the bias binding to the outside of the strap and bag. Join the bias binding at a 45-degree angle for neatness. Turn the strap over and machine sew with the binding underneath, so you can line your stitches up on top of the previous stitching, exactly ¼in (6mm) from the edge. Turn under the binding so it is a snug fit to the edge and slipstitch all round.

Blue sophistication

Metallic prints inspired by the designs of Gustav Klimt are very popular with quilters and give an exotic, Art Deco style to the bags. Metallic quilting thread and braid add sparkle.

Although blue is the main colour for my alternative fabric choice, green, turquoise, ochre, brown and orange also feature in the print, along with plenty of metallic gold highlights. By selecting a ⅜in (1cm) wide Indian plaited braid, with two double strands of orange and two of gold, those colours are emphasized in the cotton prints. The braid is quite chunky, so I positioned it ½in (1.3cm) away from the edge of the bag panels and strap, so the increased bulk didn't affect the fabric feeding under the machine foot.

Rather than simply repeat the gold in my choice of metallic quilting threads, I chose one with shaded metallic greens twisted with black for a more subtle effect. Beads and small sequins could also be used with prints like these.

Coin Purse

Making the patchwork

1 Copy and enlarge by 200 per cent the templates in Fig D and cut them
out. Using the same four fabrics used for the bag patchwork and following
the instructions on pages 78–79, make two patchwork panels with one piece
of each fabric in each panel. Using the two 6in x 4½in (15.3cm x 11.4cm)
pieces of backing and wadding (batting) and following the instructions in step
2 on page 83, quilt the two panels. Cut out one purse gusset, pin to the
11in x 3in (27.9cm x 7.6cm) backing and wadding (batting) strip and machine
quilt a few lines along the gusset. Finish by trimming the panels, machine sewing
around each panel ⅛in (3mm) from the edge and machine overlocking or
zigzagging the edge.

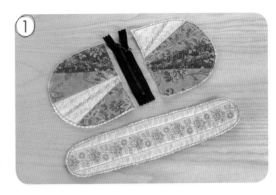

**Enlarge all templates on this page by
200 per cent**

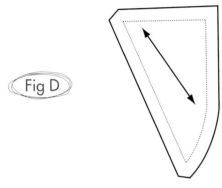

Fig D

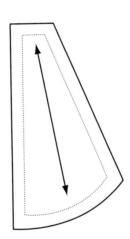

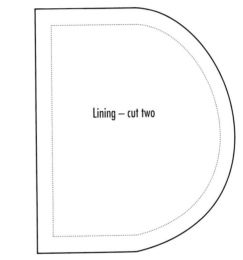

Lining – cut two

Patchwork pieces – cut two of each, plus two
more with templates flipped

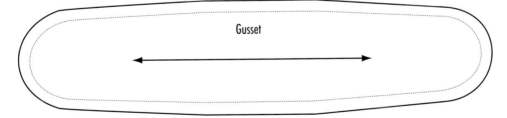

Gusset

Inserting the zip

2 Using the 4in (10.2cm) zip and one side panel, pin the zip across the
straight edge of the panel as shown, right side to right side, lining up the
edge of the panel with one edge of the zip tape and following the instructions
in steps 13–15, page 85. The zip tape needs to reach right across the top
of the purse – if it is slightly short, extend the ends by sewing two 1in x 1½in
(2.5cm x 3.8cm) pieces of patchwork fabric to each end (see the Pick and
Mix Backpack, step 10, page 114).

3 Turn the zip over and pin the matching lining panel to the other side of the zip. Tack (baste) the outer panel and lining to the zip to hold them together, if you wish. Sew the zip between the outer panel and lining using the zipper foot, stitching ¼in (6mm) from the edge. Topstitch along the sides of the zip, ⅛in (3mm) from the inside edge of the fabric strip, to neaten the fabric fold.

4 Repeat steps 2 and 3 to sew the other side panel and lining piece to the other side of the zip.

Completing the purse

5 The gusset is inserted into the purse more easily if it is sewn in several stages, so the large curve is sewn with the gusset on top and the small curve with the side panel on top. Fold the purse gusset in half to find the centre and mark this with a pin on either side. Lining sides together, align one pin with the centre seam of one patchwork side panel. Pin together. Clip the straight edge of the purse gusset ⅛in (3mm) from the edge and ease it around the curved edge of the purse panel, pinning the pieces together, as shown. Pin all around the curve and into the straight section at the side of the purse.

6 Machine sew the gusset to the purse panel. Begin at the edge of the purse on the straight side section and taper the stitching line over about ½in (1.3cm) until you are sewing ¼in (6mm) from the edge. Finish the seam by tapering the stitching line back out to the edge, again on the straight side section. Repeat for the other side of the gusset, so that both sides are sewn to the large curve at the bottom of the purse side panels.

7 Clip the purse side panel ⅛in (3mm) from the edge and ease it around the narrow curve at one end of the gusset, pinning the pieces together. Place the pins so the heads fan outwards, as shown, and can be removed as you sew. Machine sew around the curve, with the gusset on the bottom as you sew. Begin and end by overlapping the place where you tapered the other stitches out to the purse edge. Sew the remaining section of the purse and gusset seam.

8 Sew bias binding around the purse to finish (see Making bias binding page 18). Pin the bias binding to the outside of the purse. Turn the work over and machine sew with the binding underneath, so you can line your stitches up on top of the previous stitching, exactly ¼in (6mm) from the edge. Turn under the binding so it is a snug fit and slipstitch all round.

FABRIC IDEA

Vivid, sunny fabrics could be another option for these designs, with motifs in large and small scales. The fresh colours include touches of pink and green – either one could be used for a contrasting accent, perhaps with a colourful floral braid instead of lace. With a bag in these fabrics, you would rival any garden display!

Quilter's Suitcase
and Mini Pochette

Saturday is a good day for quilt workshops, and the Quilter's Suitcase is your perfect travelling companion. It is large enough to fill with dozens of fat quarters, so you can keep your workshop fabrics neatly organized. Long upholstery zips, set to one side of the bag gusset and extending right round to the base, mean the bag opens up completely, so that you can lay it flat with all your fabrics in view. Checkerboard squares and half square triangles, quilted with a grid design in multicoloured thread, make a bold but easy patchwork.

There are seven bright Japanese gold prints and vivid plain cottons in all, plus a small piece of thicker cotton for the base section. The print fabric theme continues into the lining with a large pocket for an A3-size cutting mat and your rulers, with the pocket top reinforced with a colourful ribbon braid. Leather handles complete the suitcase.

Saturday's little project

The Mini Pochette is great for rotary cutters, scissors and smaller sewing items, keeping them perfectly organized and easy to find.

Patchwork method: Checkerboard with triangle squares

A simple checkerboard shows off your fabrics when the squares aren't too small. The large triangle effect is made with triangle squares (or half square triangles), easy to make from two squares. Multicoloured quilting thread shades in and out of the fabric prints. Both sides of the bag have identical patchwork layouts. Use Fig A as a guide to help you arrange your fabric squares.

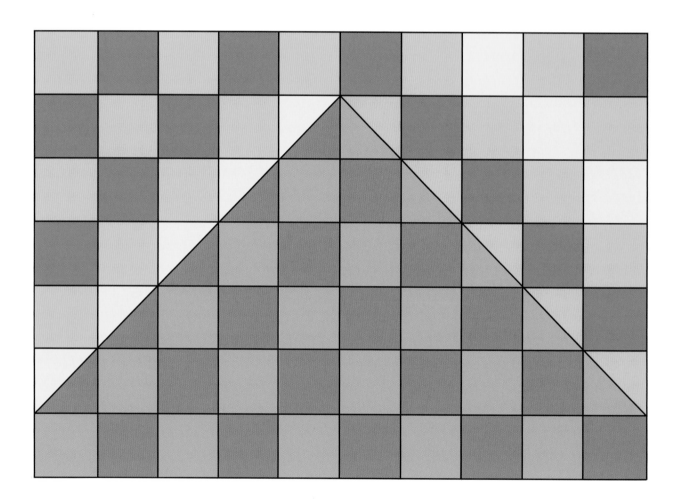

1 Reserve one small scale print for the bias binding and another fat quarter for the zip gusset. Cut one 20½in x 11½in (52.1cm x 29.2cm) piece from the largest scale print, setting this aside for the inside pocket. Cut six 2½in (6.4cm) squares and five 2⅞in (7.3cm) squares from the remainder. Choose the two boldest fabrics for the main squares and triangles in the patchwork – the dark olive striped print and plain yellow ochre are used here. Cut thirty 2½in (6.4cm) squares and five 2⅞in (7.3cm) squares from each – cut the same again from one of the remaining prints to make the patches in the large triangle section. Cut twenty-six 2½in (6.4cm) squares from the last fat quarter.

2 Make twenty triangle squares from the 2⅞in (7.3cm) squares, pairing up the large scale print with the dark (or plain) fabric you want in the triangle section and the other two fabrics together. Draw a line on the back of one of the squares in each pair. If any fabrics are striped, check the stripes are the right way up! Place the relevant squares right sides together, pin and machine sew with a ¼in (6mm) seam, lining up the edge of the machine foot with the drawn line. Repeat with another seam along the other side of the line, as shown.

3 Cut each stitched pair of squares along the drawn line as shown. Because the seam allowance is already sewn, using scissors is fine. Press the seam towards the darker fabric. Trim off the 'dog ears', the tiny triangles that stick out at the edges. Make twenty triangle squares this way.

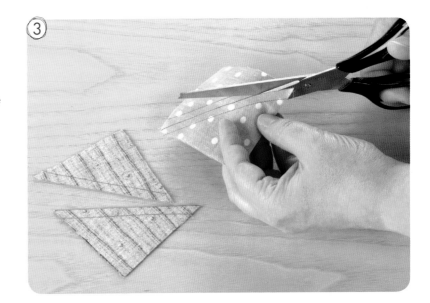

4 Using the photo and Fig A as a guide, lay out the first side panel as shown. Check that any stripes and directional fabrics are the right way up.

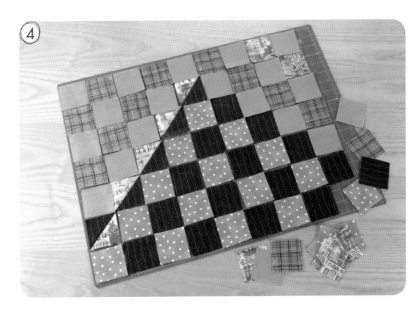

5 Using a ¼in (6mm) seam allowance, machine
sew the patches together in pairs, assembling
the patchwork in columns and chain piecing
(see page 13), following the patchwork layout
shown in Fig B. Keep the patchwork organized
by assembling each column as a series of pairs,
then sewing the pairs together into a strip of seven
squares and progressing on to the next strip.
Lay each strip in place as it is sewn.

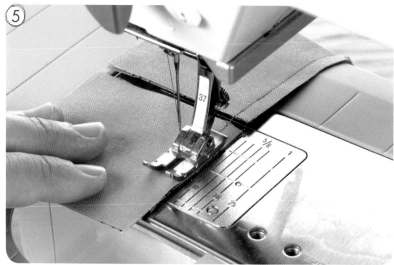

Fig B

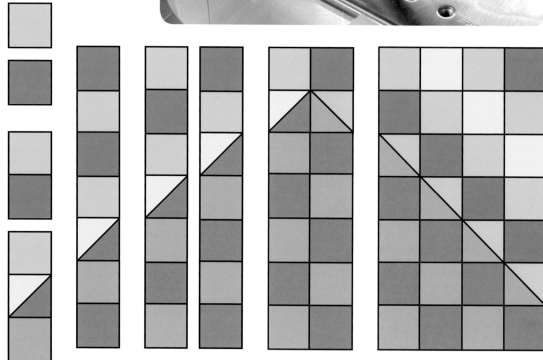

6 Press the seam allowances away from the
darker fabric and then in alternate directions.
When the strips are sewn together, the alternate
seam allowances will allow you to butt up the
seams so the corners of neighbouring squares meet
perfectly. Pin and machine sew the strips together.
Sew completed strips together in pairs and sew one
pair to another until the side panel is complete.

7 Press the seam allowances to one side across the panel, as shown. The centre seam allowance will lie better if pressed in the opposite direction, due to the triangle points meeting in the centre seam. Make another identical panel for the other side of the suitcase.

8 Using the two 21in x 15in (53.3cm x 38.1cm) pieces of calico and wadding (batting), layer the backing fabric, wadding and patchwork panel (see Making the quilt sandwich, page 14). Using the walking foot on your machine, quilt in the ditch along from side to side and up and down, so the edge of each square is quilted. Change to a shaded quilting thread and echo quilt the same lines, stitching 3/8in (1cm) from each seam line, using the width of the foot as a guide. Stitch around the panel, about 1/8in (3mm) from the edge.

FABRIC IDEA

With a larger number of fabrics, you can introduce some plains and smaller prints. Try using the dominant colours from one or more prints in the plainer fabrics or duplicate a background colour for rhythm through repetition. Strong colour and tone contrasts work well for a bold checkerboard design.

Saturday's Projects

You Will Need

- Seven fat quarters
- Plain calico backing and wadding (batting):
  - two 21in x 15in (53.3cm x 38.1cm) pieces for suitcase side panels
  - one 50in x 6in (127cm x 15.2cm) piece for suitcase gusset
  - two 9in x 5in (22.9cm x 12.7cm) pieces for pochette side panels
- One 19in x 3in (48.3cm x 7.6cm) piece of calico for pochette gusset
- Cotton quilting fabric for lining:
  - two 20½in x 14½in (52.1cm x 36.8cm) pieces for suitcase side panels
  - one 49in x 5½in (124.5cm x 14cm) piece for suitcase gusset
  - one 16½in x 5½in (41.9cm x 14cm) piece for suitcase base
  - two 8½in x 4½in (22cm x 11.4cm) pieces for pochette side panels
  - one 18¾in x 2½in (47.6cm x 6.4cm) for pochette gusset
  - one 4½in x 2½in (11.4cm x 6.4cm) piece for pochette base

- Thicker cotton for bag bases:
  - one 16½in x 5½in (41.9cm x 14cm) piece for suitcase base
  - one 4½in x 2½in (11.4cm x 6.4cm) piece for pochette base
- 100in x 1¼in (254cm x 3.2cm) bias binding
- One 20½in (52.1cm) braid or ribbon, approx. 1in (2.5cm) wide for suitcase pocket
- One 48½in (123.2cm) double pull zip, for bag – total zip tape length is 49in (124.5cm)
- One 18¼in (46.4cm) single pull zip, for purse – total zip tape length is 18¾in (47.6cm)
- One pair 13in (33cm) long leather handles
- Sewing threads to tone with patchwork
- Shaded quilting thread

Quilter's Suitcase
Making the patchwork

1 Using the diagrams and instructions on pages 94–95, make two patchwork panels for the sides of the suitcase. Setting aside the purple marble stripe for the zip gusset, use the bright yellow print for the 20½in x 11½in (52.1cm x 29.2cm) inner pocket panel and cut six 2½in (6.4cm) squares and five 2⅞in (7.3cm) squares from the remainder. Plain green replaced the plain yellow and a white print replaced the green polka dots, with thirty 2½in (6.4cm) squares and five 2⅞in (7.3cm) squares cut from each. Six 2½in (6.4cm) squares and five 2⅞in (7.3cm) squares are plain red and twenty-four 2½in (6.4cm) squares are from the red print. The final twenty-six 2½in (6.4cm) squares are a pink print. The rest of the plain red was kept for bias binding.

Layer and quilt both the panels, as described in step 8 on page 95. Trim the panels to size. Use a 2½in (6.4cm) circle template to round off each corner of each panel.

Using the diagrams and instructions on pages 94–95

TIP

The suitcase handles don't have to be exactly 13in (33cm) long, but they need to be long enough to come together comfortably over the depth of the suitcase when you carry it.

1

Making the inside pocket

2 Make the pocket panel using the 20½in x11½in (52.1cm x 29.2cm) piece of patchwork fabric and the 20½in (52.1cm) length of braid or ribbon. Turn under a ¼in (6mm) hem along the top pocket edge, turning the edge under twice to the wrong side, so the raw edge is concealed. Machine sew along the edge of the hem. Pin and sew the braid or ribbon to the right side of the panel, setting it back slightly from the fabric edge, as shown.

TIP

A non-stretchy braid or ribbon stabilizes the top edge of the pocket, so it doesn't pull out of shape when used. If you can't find a pretty braid, a plainer ribbon could be sewn to the inside edge of the pocket instead.

3 Use a 2½in (6.4cm) circle template to round off the bottom corners of the panel and all four corners of one of the 20½in x 14½in (52.1cm x 36.8cm) lining panels. Pin the pocket to the lining panel, aligning the pocket and panel edges, as shown.

Attaching the handles and lining

4 Position the leather handles, making sure that the bag panels are the right way up – the triangle design should point upwards. Use double-sided sticky tape to hold the handles in position temporarily, while you sew.

5 Hand sew the end of each handle in place (see Sewing leather handles, page 21). Select thread that matches the leather colour and stitch with a doubled, waxed thread for extra strength.

6 Place one completed side panel back to back with one 20½in x 14½in (52.1cm x 36.8cm) piece of lining fabric. Pin around the edge and trim the lining to match the curved panel corners. Shown is the lining panel with the pocket attached, so this is the top panel when the suitcase is laid open flat. Machine sew each side panel to the lining ⅛in (3mm) from the edge. Machine zigzag or overlock each panel.

Making the zip gusset

7 Cut three 5½in (14cm) strips from the fat quarter you set aside in step 1. These can be cut across the fabric or parallel to the selvedge, as you wish. Square off the shorter ends and sew the strips together to make one long strip. Cut this to measure 49in x 5½in (124.5cm x 14 cm). Using the 50in x 6in (127cm x 15.2 cm) backing and wadding (batting) pieces, make a quilt sandwich.

With the walking foot on your sewing machine, quilt with a simple, all over design – I used multicoloured quilting thread to stitch lines at right angles to the long edge of the strip. Stitch around the panel, about ⅛in (3mm) from the edge. Use a rotary cutter to trim the backing and wadding to match the edge of the strip. Cut the strip lengthwise to make one 1¼in (3.8cm) and one 4¼in (10.8cm) wide strip, both 49in (124.5cm) long. Cut the 49in x 5½in (124.5cm x 14 cm) piece of lining fabric the same way. With the 48½in (123.2cm) zip – total zip tape length is 49in (124.5cm) – follow the instructions for inserting a zip on page 17 to make a zip panel for the suitcase, as shown.

TIP

Cutting the zip panel into 1¼in (3.8cm) and 4¼in (10.8cm) wide strips means the suitcase is quite deep laid on its side and unzipped. If you want the bottom part to be shallower, cut the strip so the top section is wider than 1¼in (3.8cm).

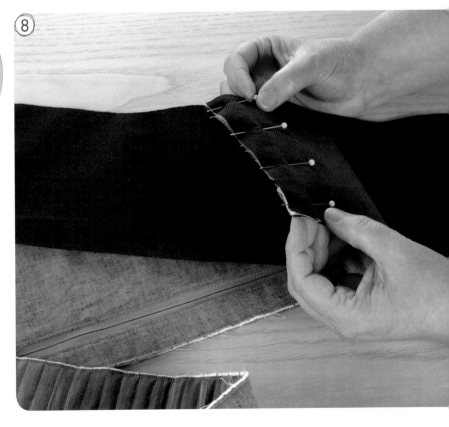

8 Pin the 16½in x 5½in (41.9cm x 14cm) panel for the suitcase base to the end of the zip strip, right sides together and pinning across the short end. Pin the corresponding piece of lining fabric with the right side against the inside of the zip strip, so the end of the zip strip is sandwiched between the suitcase base panel and the lining, as shown (I used the same fabric for the base and lining, so it didn't matter if they got swapped over now). Machine sew the pieces together using a ¼in (6mm) seam. Press the base panel and lining away from the zip strip – the seam allowance will lie this way naturally.

9 Repeat step 8 with the other end of the zip strip, base panel and lining. The ends of the zip strip will be encased in a loop between the base panel and lining, as shown. Machine overlock or zigzag the seam allowances for extra strength. Align the edges of the lining fabrics with the outer edge of the gusset and machine sew each side panel to the lining ⅛in (3mm) from the edge. The zip gusset is now complete.

TIP

Make zips to the length required from nylon coil zipper, following the instructions on page 16. You can make double pull zips, with two zip pulls to open it in opposite directions, as well as conventional single pull zips from the same length of zipper.

Completing the bag

10 Find the centre top and bottom of the gusset strip by folding the loop in half and lining up the ends of the base panel. Mark these points with a pin on the edge closest to the zip. Fold the gusset in half again to find the midpoint on the sides and mark with pins. Line up these pins with the centre top, bottom and sides of the upper side panel (with the pocket) and pin the gusset to the side panel. Continue pinning along the straight sides towards the corners. Clip the gusset strip to ease it around the side panel's curved corners, about ⅛in (3mm) from the edge. Machine sew the gusset to the side panel with a ¼in (6mm) seam allowance. Pin the other side panel in place and machine sew.

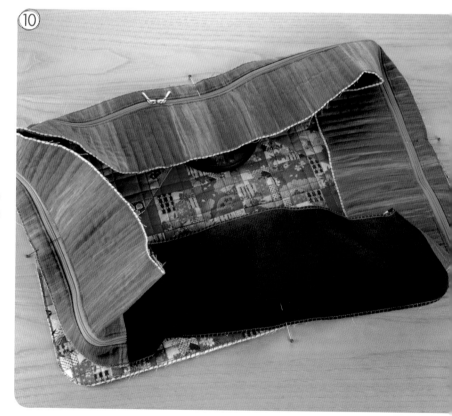

11 Make the bias binding, following the instructions on page 18. Pin the bias binding to the outside of the bag, joining the binding with a ¼in (6mm) seam on a 45-degree angle along a straight section. Ease the bias binding around the curved corners. Turn the work over and machine sew with the binding underneath, so you can line your stitches up on top of the previous stitching, exactly ¼in (6mm) from the edge. Turn under the binding so it is a snug fit to the edge and slipstitch all round.

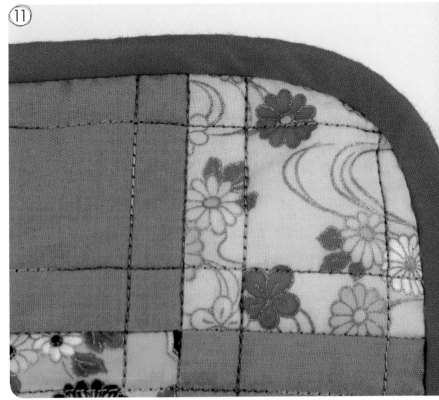

World traveller

A chic palette of green, yellow ochre and olive changes the mood for a special weekend away in a bustling city (the bag fits current airline sizes for carry-on baggage). The pochette comes in handy as a make-up bag. Using a fat quarter bundle as my starting point, I added a travel themed print, which introduced the yellow ochre accent to the green and lilac. A busy and colourful patchwork like this needs some plainer fabrics to let your eye rest a little. If you don't want to use two completely plain fabrics, as in the main colourway, try replacing one with a regular polka dots pattern or introduce fabrics with splotchy or spattered effects instead.

I kept the impact of the travel print by using it for the inner pocket, instead of the oriental print in the first bag set. The thicker woven stripe was ideal for the zip gusset and I used the same base fabric as the main colour theme.

Mini Pochette

Making the patchwork

1 Cut two 2⅞in (7.3cm) squares from four different fabrics and make eight triangle squares, following steps 2 and 3 on page 93. Cut eight 2½in (6.4cm) squares in pairs, i.e. two different fabrics for each pochette side panel. The two panels don't have to be identical. Arrange the patchwork pieces to make the panel, with four triangle squares arranged in the centre of each, as shown in Fig C. Machine sew the patches together in pairs, press, and sew the pairs together to make the patchwork panels, using a ¼in (6mm) seam allowance.

 Fig C

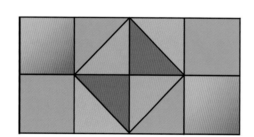 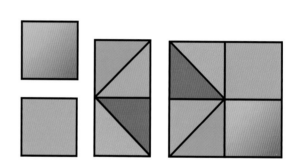

2 Using the two 9in x 5in (22.9cm x 12.7cm) pieces of calico and wadding (batting), layer the backing fabric, wadding and patchwork panel (see Making the quilt sandwich, page 14). Quilt the side panels with the same simple grid design used for the suitcase side panels (step 8, page 95). Stitch around the panel, about ⅛in (3mm) from the edge and trim the backing and wadding to match the edge of the patchwork. Use a 2½in (6.4cm) circle template to round off corners of each panel. Pin each panel back-to-back with one of the 8½in x 4½in (22cm x 11.4cm) lining pieces as shown. Stitch around the panel, about ⅛in (3mm) from the edge. Machine zigzag or overlock each panel.

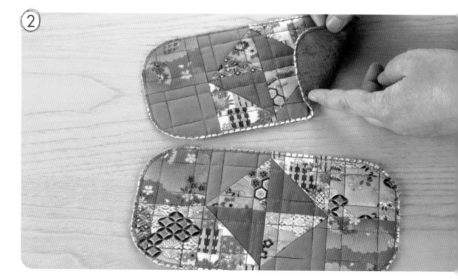

②

Making the zip gusset

3 Cut one 18¾in x 1½in (47.6cm x 3.8cm) and one 18¾in
x 1in (47.6cm x 2.5cm) strip from one of the plain fabrics.
Cut the 18¾in x 2½in (47.6cm x 6.4cm) lining fabric in two to
the same measurements. Using the 18¼in (46.4cm) single pull zip
– total zip tape length is 18¾in (47.6cm) – follow the instructions
for inserting a zip on page 17 to make a zip panel for the
pochette. Using the 4½in x 2½in (11.4cm x 6.4cm) piece of
lining fabric and a piece of patchwork fabric cut to the same size,
assemble the zip gusset following the instructions for the suitcase
zip gusset in steps 8 and 9 on pages 99–100, as shown.

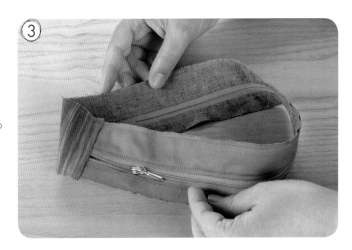

Completing the bag

4 Follow the same method for completing the suitcase in steps
10 and 11 on pages 100–101 to add the zip gusset to the
side panels and finish with bias bound edges.

FABRIC IDEA

Monochromatic colour schemes always look
sophisticated, especially prints with high
contrast. Including a mini checkerboard print
echoes the main patchwork design on a
small scale. Use a mainly black print for
the binding to frame the patchwork
solidly. You could introduce a touch of
colour with your quilting thread or the
bag handles – red would look chic.

Pick and Mix Backpack
and Ticket Pocket

Sunday's Pick and Mix Backpack is an ideal size for travel hand baggage. It has two main compartments, one with an extra inner pocket, so you don't have to unpack everything to find one item at the bottom. There are two large zip pockets on the front and the secret zip pocket in the back panel is inaccessible when the backpack is worn. The zip strips join the patchwork panels together, three on the front and two on the back.

My bundle of eight fat quarters in warm colours was accented with red webbing on the adjustable padded straps, fastened with red plastic side release buckles. Strips and squares joined into long strings of fabric give the foundation-pieced patchwork a random effect. I added extra quilting with cross-hatched lines in a shaded thread all over the patchwork. The bag base is tough denim.

This is quite a complex bag to make and I would advise completing one of the earlier projects in the book before attempting this one.

Sunday's little project

The backpack is the most challenging bag in the book but the matching Ticket Pocket is a piece of cake. Large enough for most tickets, passports and boarding passes, it can be stowed in the backpack's secret pocket when not required.

Patchwork method: Foundation piecing with pieced strips

Using a number of coordinated fabrics with one accent fabric and piecing the strips creates a more complex version of the foundation piecing first used for the Strippy Bag (page 24). By stitching the patchwork in several sections, joined by the zips and pockets, the strips can slant in different directions. Extra quilting with an all-over variable grid stiffens the panels, while the shaded thread helps harmonise the fabrics.

Making the patchwork foundation

1 Using tracing paper and the diagram for the back of the backpack, Fig A, draft a pattern for the foundation panels. Use 12in (30.5cm) and 2½in (6.4cm) diameter cardboard circles to mark the curves. First, draft the outline of Fig A, drawing the red line down the centre and taking measurements at right angles across that. Trace two outline copies – one to keep for the lining pattern and one to use as the outline for the front panel pattern in Fig B (see step 2). On the original pattern, mark the dashed line 4in (10.2cm) from the top of the panel and the second dashed line 1in (2.5cm) below that. Cut the pattern along the *second* dashed line from the top – labelled 'zip is inserted along dashed line below.'

TIP
Draft the pattern by placing your cutting mat under the tracing paper, so you have a grid to follow as you draw.

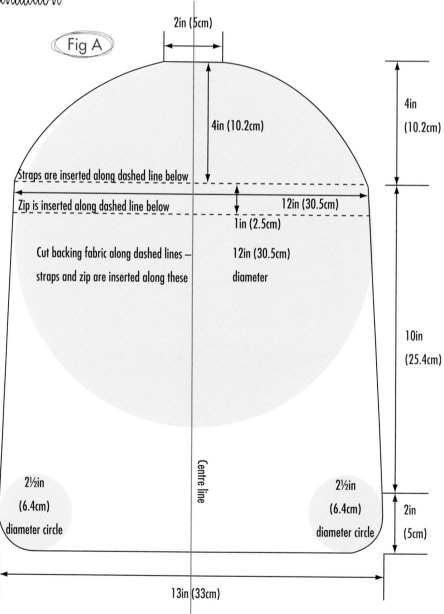

Fig A

2in (5cm)

4in (10.2cm)

4in (10.2cm)

Straps are inserted along dashed line below

12in (30.5cm)

Zip is inserted along dashed line below

1in (2.5cm)

Cut backing fabric along dashed lines – straps and zip are inserted along these

12in (30.5cm) diameter

10in (25.4cm)

2½in (6.4cm) diameter circle

2½in (6.4cm) diameter circle

Centre line

2in (5cm)

13in (33cm)

2 Use one copy of the traced outline to draft the front panel pattern, shown in Fig B. Use the 45-degree angle on your quilter's ruler to position the upper dashed line that intersects the centre vertical line (shown in red) 2½in (6.4cm) from the top of the panel. The second dashed line is at right angles to the first one, intersecting the centre vertical line 1in (2.5cm) below the first dashed line. Cut the pattern along both dashed lines, so there are three pieces. Use these and the pattern pieces from step 1 to cut one set of pieces for the front panel and one for the back from two 16in x 13in (40.6cm x 33cm) pieces of calico and wadding (batting). For the front panel only, flip over each piece of calico so they are mirror images of the pattern pieces. For the front and back panel foundation, pin each piece of calico to the wadding (batting) and use it as a template to rotary cut the straight edges. Cut the corner curves with scissors.

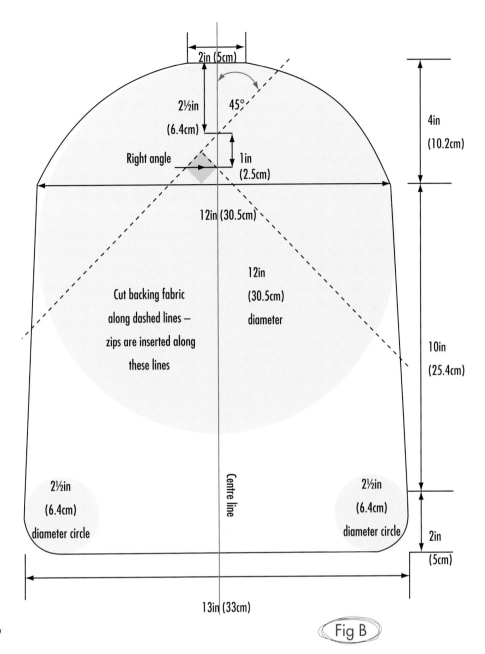

2in (5cm)

2½in (6.4cm)

45°

Right angle

1in (2.5cm)

12in (30.5cm)

12in (30.5cm) diameter

Cut backing fabric along dashed lines — zips are inserted along these lines

4in (10.2cm)

10in (25.4cm)

2½in (6.4cm) diameter circle

2½in (6.4cm) diameter circle

2in (5cm)

Centre line

13in (33cm)

Making the patchwork

Fig B

3 Reserving one fabric for the bias binding strips and selecting the one with the highest contrast for the 1½in (3.8cm) squares, cut three 1½in (3.8cm) strips across the width of the other six fabrics and square off the ends, removing the selvedge. The strips will be approximately 21in (53.3cm) long. Cut one 12in x 14in (30.5cm x 35.6cm) piece for the inner pocket from the contrast fabric and cut fifteen 1½in (3.8cm) squares from the remainder. Machine sew one square to one end of fifteen of the 1½in (3.8cm) strips, then sew the strips together to make three long strips with one piece of each fabric in each strip and the pieces separated by squares. Press seams away from the squares. Turn over the largest front panel foundation piece, so the wadding (batting) is on top, and replace the pins. Lay the end of one strip across the panel at an angle that is not parallel to any of the edges, cut to length and pin, as shown.

3

4 Pin another strip on top of the first strip, right
sides together. Machine sew patchwork,
through both strips and the foundation, using ¼in
(6mm) seam.

5 Flip over the second strip and finger press
open, running your finger firmly along the
seam. Pin the third strip down to hold it in place,
arranging the pinheads along the raw edge, so you
can remove them when the next strip is pinned.

6 Continue adding more strips the same way,
until the whole panel is covered. Cutting
pieces from all the long patchwork strips in turn will
help you maintain variety for a random look. It looks
best if you don't allow the contrast squares to touch
each other in adjacent strips.

7 The two upper front panels are sewn from
the straight edge outwards, like the Strippy
Handbag side panels (page 28). Arrange the strips
so that obviously one way patterns, like the ships
and animals here, are the right way up. Machine
sew one strip to the straight edge of the panel,
about ⅛in (3mm) from the edge before adding
more strips.

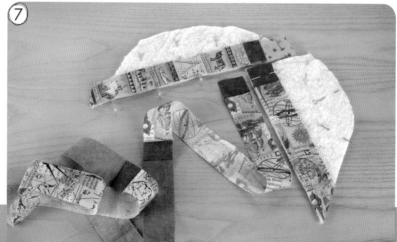

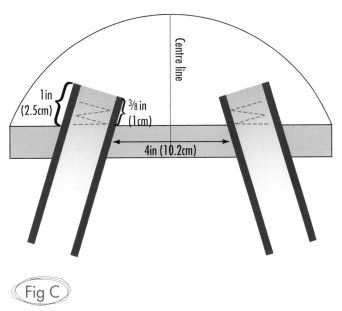

Centre line

1in
(2.5cm)

³/8 in
(1cm)

4in (10.2cm)

Fig C

8 The padded straps (see page 110) are sewn to the top section of the back panel after the first strip is positioned, as shown. Machine sew the strip to the straight edge of the panel, about ¹/8in (3mm) from the edge, then position and pin the straps with the *back* of the straps on top, lining them up with the top edge of the first patchwork strip as shown in Fig C. Machine sew back and forth across the top of the straps, as shown by the red dashed lines.

9 Pin another strip on top of the first strip, right sides together, and machine sew. Flip over the second strip and finger press open, running your finger firmly along the seam. Continue adding strips until the panel is complete. Turn each panel over and machine stitch around the edge, about ¹/8in (3mm) away from the edge. Trim the overhanging strips to match the backing panel, using your ruler and rotary cutter whenever possible.

Quilting

10 Change to a multicoloured quilting thread. With the walking foot on your machine, quilt a single line across one panel, without following any of the lines in the patchwork, curving the line slightly. Quilt lines parallel to the first, working outwards across the panel and using the width of the machine foot as a guide by lining up the previous stitch line against the side of the foot. When the panel is covered in lines going in one direction, stitch a line going across the first set of lines and repeat the procedure. The shapes created by the grid will change proportion across the panel, giving a sense of movement.

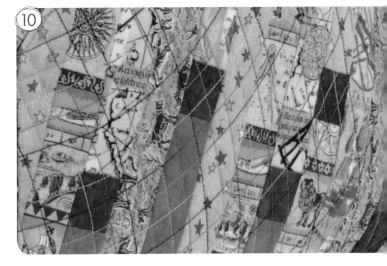

Sunday's Projects

You Will Need

- Eight fat quarters
- Plain calico backing and wadding (batting):
    two 16in x 13in (40.6cm x 33cm) pieces for backpack panels
    one 14½in x 5in (36.8cm x 13.7cm) piece for pocket side panel
- Two 24in x 2in (61cm x 5cm) strips of wadding (batting) for backpack straps
- Cotton quilting fabric for lining and outer pockets:
    two 16in x 13in (40.6cm x 33cm) pieces for backpack panels
    three 16in x 13in (40.6cm x 33cm) pieces for backpack outer pockets
    one 16in x 13in (40.6cm x 33cm) piece for backpack lining divider
    two 32½in x 4in (82.6cm x 10.2cm) pieces for backpack zip gusset
    two 17½in x 4in (44.5cm x 10.2cm) pieces for backpack gusset base
    one 14½in x 5in (37cm x 11.4cm) pieces for ticket pocket lining
- One 17½in x 7½in (44.5cm x 19cm) piece of denim for backpack base

- Bias binding (see Making bias binding, page 18):
    one 140in x 1¼in (355.6cm x 3.2cm) wide strip
    one 98in x 1in (248.9cm x 2.5cm) wide strip
- Two 32in (81.3cm) double pull zips for backpack – total zip tape length is 32½in (82.6cm)
- Single pull zips:
    one 8in (20.3cm) zip, for backpack front pocket (tape length 21.6cm)
    two 10in (25.4cm) zips, for backpack front and back pockets (tape length 26.7cm)
- Webbing, 1in (2.5cm) wide, for backpack:
    two 32in (81.3cm) pieces for straps
    two 3in (7.6cm) pieces for side tabs
- Two side release buckles or tri-glide buckles to fit webbing width, for backpack
- One 2in (5cm) strip of hook and loop tape for ticket pocket (optional)
- Sewing threads to tone with patchwork
- Shaded quilting thread
- Three pieces of tracing paper, larger than 16in x 13in

Pick and Mix Backpack
Making the straps

1 Select two of the patchwork fabrics and piece together two 24in x 2in (61cm x 5cm) strips from each fabric using diagonal seams. Make a quilt sandwich by placing one fabric strip face down, place one 24in x 2in (61cm x 2cm) wadding (batting) strip along that and the other strip right side up, pinning through all the layers. Mark a curve around the bottom corner with a 2in (5cm) circle and cut to shape. Machine sew around the edge, about ⅛in (3mm) away from the edge. Pin and machine sew the 1in (2.5cm) wide bias binding around the edge. As shown in Fig D, pin and machine sew one 32in (81.3cm) piece of 1in (2.5cm) wide webbing down the centre of each strap, starting at the top and stitching 1/16in (1mm) from the edge. Stitch a figure of eight reinforcement at the bottom of the strap, before finishing off by stitching the other side of the webbing.

Fig D

Making the patchwork

2 Following the instructions on pages 108–109, make the patchwork panels, inserting the straps into the back panel as shown in steps 8 and 9. Use the fabric with most contrast for the 1½in (3.8cm) squares – the hot orange print is used here – and cut one 12in x 14in (30.5cm x 35.6cm) piece of this for the inner pocket. Quilt the panels, as described in step 10 on page 109. Make the bias binding (see page 19) with one 140in x 1¼in (355.6cm x 3.2cm) wide strip for binding the backpack and one 98in x 1in (248.9cm x 2.5cm) wide strip for binding the edges of the straps.

Cutting out the pocket linings

3 Using the three 16in x 13in (40.6cm x 33cm) lining pieces for the backpack outer pockets and the paper pattern used to cut the front and back panel foundation pieces, cut the pocket linings, using Fig E as a guide. The dashed lines correspond to the way the foundation panels were cut in step 2 on page 107. Cut one front panel into three pieces, the same as the foundation panel, but cut the second front panel into only *two* pieces, along dashed line C to D in the diagram and discard piece B from this set. Cut the back panel along dashed line F to G, the same way the foundation panel was cut.

TIP

The back of the main bag lining will be visible as the back of the largest pocket on each side. Use a lining fabric that is attractive on both sides or use a plain fabric or batik where both sides are the same.

Fig E

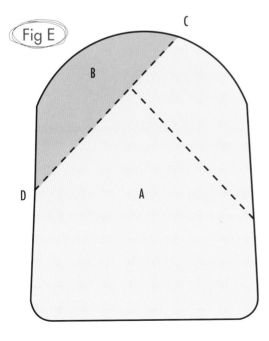

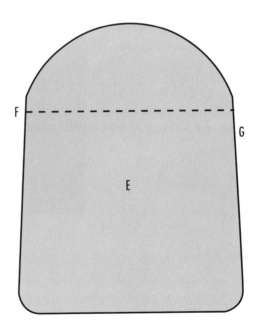

Making the zip strips

4 The three shorter zips have pieces of patchwork
fabric sewn to the ends, to reduce bulk in the
bag construction seams. If you are using ready-made
zips, use these pieces to extend the zip to meet the
bag requirements. Make the zip strips longer than
required and cut each strip to length as it is inserted.
Cut twelve 2in x 1in (5cm x 2.5cm) pieces of fabric,
four for each zip. Pin one piece on the back and one
piece on the front of the end of the zip, as shown in
diagram 4, right sides against the zip, and machine
sew using ¼in (6mm) seam. Flip the strips outwards
and finger press. Pin or tack (baste) them in place.
Repeat for the other end of the zip.

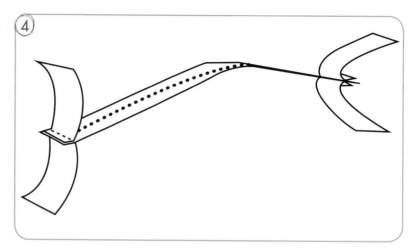

Making the back panel

5 Insert the zip between the two pieces of
the back panel the same way as sewing the
zip in the Strippy Bag, steps 7–9 on page 30.
Using the bottom half of the back and the relevant
piece of pocket lining cut out in step 3 (page 111),
attach the zip strip to the lower part of the back
panel first, centering the zip strip against the back
panel and trimming the strip ends to match. Press
and topstitch the fabric along the side of each
inserted zip during construction.

Before attaching the upper part of the back
panel and back pocket lining the same way, make
a flap to cover the zip to prevent it snagging your
clothes. Cut a 12in x 2in (30.5cm x 5cm) strip of
any patchwork fabric, fold in half lengthwise and
machine sew along the fold, ⅛in (3mm) from the
edge. Tack (baste) the raw edge of the strip across
the upper edge of the zip. Continue to sew the zip
into the upper part of the back panel, sandwiching
the flap between the back panel and the zip.
When the bag is assembled, the flap will be caught
in place at the side seams, covering the zip. Pin and
tack (baste) the lining panel back to back with the
back panel.

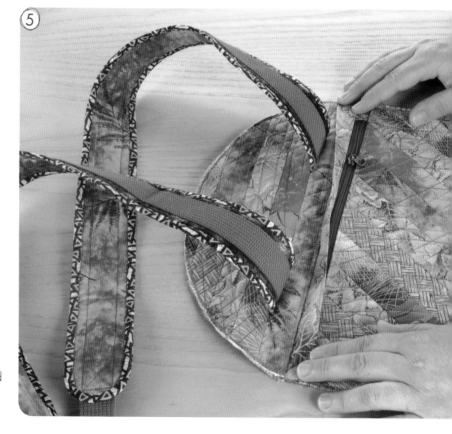

Making the front panel

6 Insert the lower zip first, using the lower front panel and the relevant piece of pocket lining, as for the back panel but without the covering flap. Once the zip is sewn between the first panel and pocket lining, pin, tack (baste) and stitch the smaller upper right panel and its lining piece. Press and topstitch the fabric along the side of each inserted zip during construction. Sew the second zip to the panel, using the corresponding larger pocket lining piece – this will be the back of the first pocket and the front of the second one. After this step, there will be two layers of fabric behind the panel, as shown.

7 Finish the front panel pockets by sewing the remaining front top piece and its lining to the upper edge of the second zip, as shown.

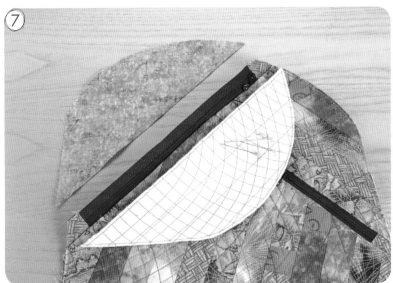

8 Pin the edges of the pockets to line up with the edges of the front panel. Pin and tack (baste) the lining panel back to back with the back panel, as shown. There will be three layers of pocket lining/lining behind the lower edge of the panel and two behind the upper left edge. Machine sew about 1/8in (3mm) away from the edge. Machine overlock or zigzag around the edge of both back and front panels, to compress the bulk of the extra lining layers at the edges.

Making the inner pocket

9 Turn under a ¼in (6mm) hem along one long side of the 12in x 14in (30.5cm x 35.6cm) inner pocket fabric, press and turn under another 1in (2.5cm) to make a deep hem across the top of the pocket. Machine sew across the top five times, sewing a scant ⅛in (3mm) from the top edge, along the folded hem edge and three more times in between. Start with the centre stitching line and sew another equidistant between the top and bottom. Using a 2½in (6.4cm) circle template, draw and cut a curve at the bottom corners.

Cut the lining divider from the remaining 16in x 13in (40.6cm x 33cm) lining fabric (I used plain fabric). Pin the inner pocket to the lining divider, with the corners and side edges aligned. The pocket base is wider than the divider, so make a small pleat on either side to take up the excess, just after coming around the corner curve, as shown pinned.

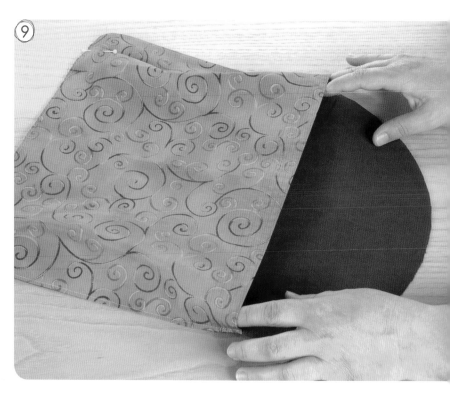

Making the zip panels

10 Piece together two 32½in x 4in (82.6cm x 10.5cm) strips from two of the remaining fabrics, one for each strip. Taper these as indicated in Fig F (not to scale), folding each strip in half across the length and tapering one side from 4in (10.2cm) at the end to 2¾in (7cm) in the middle. Shape the two 32½in x 4in (82.6cm x 10.2cm) strips of lining fabric the same way. Cut a 1in (2.5cm) wide strip from the *non* tapered side of each of these four panels.

Using one 1in (2.5cm) wide outer strip and one 1in (2.5cm) lining strip, insert one 32in (81.3cm) double pull zip between the fabric and lining (see Inserting zips, page 17). Then insert the zip between the tapered pieces of fabric and lining, making sure you stitch the zip to the *non* tapered side. Press and topstitch the fabric along the side of the zip. Pin the fabric and lining edge together and machine sew along the edge, about ⅛in (3mm) away from the edge. Make two zip panels this way.

Fig F — 4in (10.2cm) — fold — 2¾in (7cm)

Assembling the zip gussets and lining divider

11 Place one 17½in x 4in (44.5cm x 10.2cm) piece of lining and one zip panel right sides together along the end and pin. Machine sew with a ¼in (6mm) seam. Machine overlock or zigzag the seam allowance. Repeat with the other end of the lining piece and zip panel, to make one zip gusset. Repeat with the other lining piece and zip panel, as shown.

12 Find the centre top and bottom of one gusset strip by folding the loop in half and lining up the ends of the base panel. Mark the centre top and bottom with a pin on the *non* tapered side, i.e. the edge closest to the zip. Fold the lining divider in half lengthwise and mark the centre of the top and bottom edges with a pin. Line up the pins on the zip gusset with the pins on the lining divider and pin the gusset to the side panel, as shown. Continue pinning along the base towards the corners. Clip the zip gusset to ease it around the lining divider's curved corners, about ⅛in (3mm) from the edge and around the curved top of the lining. Pin all round, as shown.

TIP

With numerous pieces for pockets and a more complicated lining, this is a challenging bag. For a simplified version, omit all the outer pockets (and their linings), joining the quilted patchwork panels with 1in (2.5cm) wide sashing strips instead.

13 Turn the panel over and repeat with the other zip gusset, so there is one zip gusset pinned to each side of the lining divider. Make sure the ends of the zip sections are lining up on either side of the divider. Machine sew the gusset to the lining divider with a ¼in (6mm) seam allowance. Machine overlock or zigzag the seam allowance you have just sewn. Using the 1¼in (3.2cm) bias binding strip, bias bind the seam. Tack (baste) the bias bound seam allowance at each end, so it lies towards the front of the backpack – decide if you want the internal pocket in the front or the back main section of the bag and tack the ends of the bound seam accordingly.

14 Overlock or zigzag the edge of the 17½in x 7½in (44.5cm x 19cm) piece of denim. Right sides together, pin the end of the denim panel to the end of the zip gussets on one side of the backpack. The denim should lie in the same direction as the zip gusset. Turn the backpack over so you can see the seam allowance joining the zip gussets to the base lining and position the pins on this side. Machine sew the denim panel to the backpack along this line, starting at the outside edge of the zip gusset and following the previous seam line, as far as the zip. Repeat from the other outside edge of the zip gusset. The centre sections must be hand sewn with small hem stitches.

Completing the bag

15 Make two side tabs for the backpack buckles using the two 3in (7.6cm) pieces of 1in (2.5cm) wide webbing. Cut two 2⅞in x 2½in (7.3cm x 6.4cm) pieces from one of the patchwork fabrics. Fold each of these in half along the longest side and machine sew along the edge to make a tube measuring 2½in (6.4cm long). Press the seam open. Thread the slot part of one side-release buckle (or the tri-glide buckle) on to one piece of webbing and hold the ends together. With the fabric tube inside out, insert the ends of the webbing into the tube and machine sew across, ½in (1.3cm) from the end, as shown by the red dashed line in diagram 15. Sew back and forth several times and finish by stitching zigzag across the end. Turn the tube right side out, by sliding the fabric back over where you have just stitched. Topstitch across the join between the tube and the webbing, ⅛in (3mm) from the stitched end of the tube.

16 Pin and tack (baste) one buckle tab to either side of the completed back panel, with the lower edge of the tab positioned 2in (5cm) up the side of the back panel. Repeating the pin marking method described in step 12, page 115, line up and pin the centre section to the back panel, with the linings facing each other, so the seam will be on the outside. Machine sew the seam with a ¼in (6mm) seam allowance and machine overlock or zigzag the seam. Pin and machine sew the front panel to the backpack centre section, following the same procedure for attaching the back panel. Using the 1¼in (3.2cm) bias binding strip, bias bind both these seams (see page 18). If you are using side release buckles, thread one buckle section on to each of the straps and fasten to the buckle tabs. For tri-glide buckles, simply thread the strap through the buckle on each side.

⑯

TIP

Give the backpack a firmer base by backing the denim with heavy iron-on interfacing, cut ½in (1.3cm) smaller than the panel all round.

Sail away

Be the captain on a voyage of exploration! Four very busy prints, featuring ships, antique maps, compasses, exotic animals and script plus one mottled mid blue and another with tiny stars are the selection used for the patchwork strips, all very similar in colour and value. Two fabrics have a one way pattern, so I arranged them with the motifs upwards.

The red print provides the stronger contrast for the squares and livens up the patchwork, so consider where these squares are placed — you should achieve a random but balanced distribution over the bag panels. The eighth print is much darker and has a faux-woven design, which looked good on a 45-degree angle, so it was ideal for the bias binding.

Ticket Pocket

Making the patchwork

1 Following the patchwork method on pages 107–108,
make one 14½in x 5in (37cm x 11.4cm) patchwork panel
for the ticket pocket, making a foundation from the 14½in x 5in
(36.8cm x 13.7cm) backing and wadding (batting). Quilt the
panel with the variable grid design, as in step 10 on page 109.
Trim the panel and machine sew around the panel, about ⅛in
(3mm) away from the edge. Machine overlock or zigzag the panel.

Making the bag

2 Fold the patchwork strip in half so the bottom of the bag is
on a fold. Mark a curve around the bottom corners using a
1½in (3.8cm) circle template and cut around the curve. Fold, mark
and cut the 14½in x 5in (37cm x 11.4cm) ticket pocket lining the
same way. If you want to add a hook and loop tape fastener,
do it now (see Tip). Machine sew the side seams of the pocket
with a ¼in (6mm) seam allowance, following around the curves
at the bottom. Sew the lining side seams with the same seam
allowance, but leave about 3in (7.5cm) unsewn in one side seam,
as shown. Press the seams open. Turn the patchwork pocket right
side out but leave the lining turned inside out.

TIP
*For a simple closure, use a
2in (5cm) strip of hook and loop tape,
centering it on the lining accross the top, so
it closes neatly.*

Making the strap

3 Make a ¾in (1.9cm) wide strap following the instructions for
making an open end strap on page 19. Use a 3in x 51½in
(7.6cm x 131.8cm) strip folded in four lengthwise. Pin one end
of the strap to the top of one side of the pocket, as shown, as far
to the side as possible without crossing the side seam. Line up
the end of the strap with the top of the pocket. Taking care not to
twist the strap, pin the other end of the strap to the other side of
the pocket, so the strap will be attached to the opposite ends on
opposite sides of the pocket.

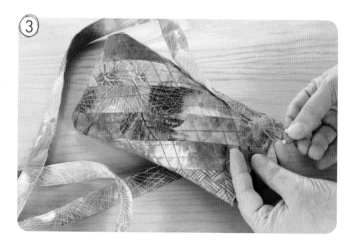

Completing the bag

4 Place the outer patchwork pocket inside the bag lining – the strap will be hidden between the two. Align the side seams on the bag and the lining, line up the tops of both and pin around the top, as shown. Machine sew around the top of the pocket, stitching the lining to the outside of the pocket and stitching through the strap ends.

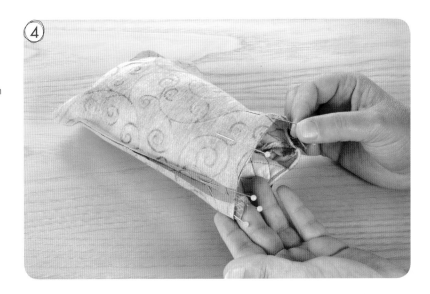

Assembling the zip gussets and lining divider

5 Slip your fingers inside the gap in the lining seam and take hold of the bag outer. Carefully turn the whole bag right sides out through the gap in the lining seam. When the bag is turned through, push the lining back down into the bag, making sure the corners are well turned out. By hand, slipstitch the lining gap closed. Machine sew around the top of the bag, ⅛in (3mm) from the edge.

FABRIC IDEA

A bumper bundle of Japanese fabrics including florals and geometrics takes the blue and red colour scheme off in a different direction. The blues are darker and more intense, so this time the fabric with the white background (second from right) would make the best contrast for the squares, with the red used for the binding. There are nine fat quarters in this collection, so you could use the second white-based print (in the middle of the bundle) for some of the lining pieces.

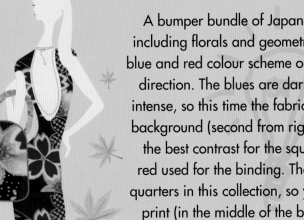

Suppliers

Fabrics, notions and equipment like those used in this book are available from the following retailers:

UK

The African Fabric Shop
19 Hebble Mount
Meltham, Holmfirth
West Yorkshire, HD9 4HG
tel: 01484 850 188
email: magie@africanfabric.co.uk
www.africanfabric.co.uk
African fabrics and trims

Antique Angel
21 Thomas More buildings
10 Ickenham Road
Ruislip, HA4 7BA
tel: 07765 888136
email: kylie@antiqueangel.co.uk
www.antiqueangel.co.uk
Sepia & country fabric ranges; zips and bag fittings

The Button Lady
16 Hollyfield Road South
Sutton Coldfield
W Midlands, B76 1NX
tel: 0121 329 3234
www.thebuttonlady.co.uk
Buttons, clasps, charms, beads and sequins

The Cotton Patch
1285 Stratford Road
Hall Green,Birmingham
B28 9AJ
tel: 0121 702 2840
email: mailorder@cottonpatch.net
www.cottonpatch.co.uk
Fabrics (including woven stripes) and patchwork supplies

Defnydd Melanie Fabrics
The Old Exchange Stores
Capel Bangor
Aberystwyth
Ceredigion, SY23 3LT
tel: 01970 880811
www.melaniefabrics.co.uk
Patchwork supplies

Euro Japan Links Limited
32 Nant Road
Childs Hill
London, NW1 2AT
tel: 020 8201 9324
email: eurojpn@aol.com
www.eurojapanlinks.co.uk
Japanese fabrics & threads (internet & mail order only)

Hannah's Room
50 Church Street
Brierley, Barnsley
South Yorkshire, S72 9HT
tel: 01226 713427
email: sales@hannahsroom.co.uk
www.hannahsroom.co.uk
Batik fabrics

Kaleidoscope of Colour
Dobbies Garden Centre
Boclair Road
Milgavnie, G62 6EP
tel: 01360 622815
email: customer.care@kalquilts.com
www.kalquilts.com
Fabrics and notions

Patchwork Corner
51 Belswains Lane
Hemel Hempstead
Hertfordshire, HP3 9PW
tel: 01442 259000
email: jenny@patchworkcorner.co.uk
www.patchworkcorner.com
Fabrics and notions

USA

The City Quilter
133 West 25th Street
New York
NY 10001
tel: 212-807-0390
email: info@cityquilter.com
www.cityquilter.com
Fabrics & quilting supplies

eQuilter.com
5455 Spine Road, Suite E
Boulder
CO 80301
tel: USA Toll Free: 877-FABRIC-3
or: 303-527-0856
email: service@equilter.com
www.eQuilter.com
Patchwork fabrics

Hancocks of Paducah
3841 Hinkleville Rd
Paducah
KY 42001
tel: USA Toll Free 1-800-845-8723
International 1-270-443-4410
email: customerservice@hancocks-paducah.com
www.hancocks-paducah.com
Fabrics & quilting supplies

Jo-Ann Stores inc.
5555 Darrow Road
Hudson
OH 44236
tel: 1-888-739-4120
email: guestservices@jo-annstores.com
www.joann.com
General needlework and quilting supplies (mail order and stores across the USA)

Acknowledgments

I would like to thank the following for their help with sourcing materials – Magie at the African Fabric Shop, Kylie at Antique Angel, the Button Lady, Melanie at Defnydd Melanie Fabrics, Mary and Shiro at Euro Japan Links, Susan at Kaleidoscope, Jenny at Patchwork Corner, Donna and Holly at Lakehouse Dry Goods (extra fabrics for the Typo Satchel), Yasuko Okazaki and staff at Clover, and Dot Sherlock at Quilter's Needs for extra fat quarter bundles. Many thanks to my family and friends, and a big 'thank you' to our designers, photographers and editorial team at David & Charles for turning my bag designs into another colourful book!

Index